LOVE ON THE BEAT

SERGE GAINSBOURG, TRANSLATED

WALTER DUBOIS

ISBN: 978-0-578-72839-1

Walter Dubois
Houston, Texas
loveonthebeatbook@gmail.com

Cover and interior design by Tami Boyce
www.tamiboyce.com

To my wife, Eszter – thank you for always believing in this project.
Nagyon szeretlek, örökké

To my parents Ann & Alain, and to my sister Sydney
À mon ami Alexandre Tambou-Rayalou
En hommage à Serge Gainsbourg

FOREWORD

STRUCTURE

The songs have been arranged in chronological order across a dozen chapters, each prefaced by an introduction and reflecting a different period in Gainsbourg's life. The book can be read as a biography or consulted as a reference. For an immersive experience, one might consider reading the translations in chronological order while simultaneously listening to the recordings.

TRANSLATION

Remaining faithful to the original lyrics' meaning was of paramount importance. Although efforts were made to conserve them where possible, rhyme and rhythm should be experienced by listening to the recording — these translations are not meant to be sung. Annotations were used to convey meaning and highlight nuance. A short introduction precedes each translation, affording the reader an idea of the context in which the song originally came to light.

TYPOGRAPHY

In the lyrics, italic print designates spoken word, whereas bold text denotes the chorus.

COPYRIGHT

Copyright ownership of the original lyrics is indicated after each song.

COVER ART

The back cover is based on a photograph taken by Andrew Birkin of Serge and his beloved English bull terrier, Nana. Gainsbourg loved the dog because she was a present from Jane Birkin and because her face reminded him of his own. He was distraught when Nana died in July 1978, immediately ordering: "Call a carpenter. Have a casket made of the finest spruce and have a copper plate engraved with the words 'Nana Gainsbourg' affixed to it."[1] *Serge cried himself to sleep on Nana's bed that night.*[2]

REFERENCES

Two works are cited liberally throughout:

- *L'intégrale Gainsbourg: L'histoire de toutes ses chansons, Picaud et Verlant, 2011, Points*
    - *A single asterisk (*) serves to denote passages derived from this work*
- *Serge Gainsbourg: L'intégrale et cætera, édition établie par Bouvier et Vincendet, 2009, Bartillat*
    - *A double asterisk (**) serves to denote passages derived from this work*

I owe the authors a debt of gratitude for these meticulously researched reference books. Special thanks to Yves-Ferdinand Bouvier, with whom I corresponded during the translation process.

Walter Dubois
June 21ˢᵗ, 2020

---

1 Gainsbourg ou la provocation permanente, Salgues, **1989**, Jean-Claude Lattès.
2 Gainsbourg in time, Verlant, **February 2001**, Gala Magazine.

TABLE OF CONTENTS

THE BLUE PERIOD

Serge Gainsbourg's first forays into songwriting were not met with immediate success. True, he landed a record deal with Philips in 1958. True, his first album – *Du chant à la une* – won the Grand Prix du Disque in 1959, showing that critics sensed big things were in store for the thirty-year-old artist. However, audiences were slow to come to the same realization. Perhaps the lack of sustained popular success could be attributed to Serge's music being entirely dissimilar to what was being produced at the time. A passage from the biography written by Gilles Verlant: "Right away, because of his style, Gainsbourg sets himself apart from everything else out there, from all the other singers that people are talking about. There is no common ground between him and Brassens[1], Brel[2], Clay[3], or Lemarque[4]. There's a virtual abyss separating Serge from the Rive Gauche. On that side of the Seine, people are poetic and engaged, and they practice a witty and subtle form of irony. With Gainsbourg, the words, which meld with the music, are not simply grafted onto a score because they conveniently match the rhythm or harmonic structure. And they are ultra-pessimistic. With Gainsbourg, it's about sarcasm, not irony. Technically, since his very first songs, Serge refuses to follow the classic tricks of the trade: practicing scales, forcing himself to develop dramatic effects, etc. And he 'sings in the style of the time, very French, like he has a mouthful of marbles', as Eddy Mitchell[5] so beautifully puts it. He avoids rolling his R's like Barbara[6] or Brassens [...]."[7]

Indubitably, Serge's stage presence, or lack thereof, also slowed his ascent to superstar status. His looks were constantly criticized in the press, and Serge appeared to be very sensitive to the insults, so much so that he was terrified to perform onstage. "Rare press clippings from the day confirm this impression. From *Les Beaux-Arts Bruxelles,* we read the following: 'We know his songs. He sings them himself in that reedy voice of his, without any gesturing. He gives the impression of being both melancholic and indifferent, with those dreamy eyes and ears like a flying elephant.' From Paris, in *L'Officiel des spectacles:* 'Gainsbourg writes exquisite songs and sings them quite badly, just as

---

1   Georges Brassens (1921-1981) was a French poet, singer and songwriter.

2   Jacques Brel (1929-1978) was a Belgian singer-songwriter. He was also an actor and filmmaker.

3   Philippe Clay (1927-2007) was a French singer and actor.

4   Francis Lemarque (1917-2002) was a French singer-songwriter. He is perhaps best remembered for his classic song *À Paris.*

5   Eddy Mitchell (1942-) is a French singer and actor.

6   Barbara (1930-1997) was a French singer-songwriter and actress. Her poetry and mellifluous voice won her legions of fans.

7   Gainsbourg, Verlant, **2000**, Albin Michel. Translation by Paul Knobloch.

tradition would have it. He's scrawny and feeble and always seems to be a breath away from fainting or simply vanishing.' In *Arts*, from a story titled 'Gainsbourg, even uglier than Clay,' this especially harsh description can be found: 'Ears shoot out perpendicular to the head, enormous eyelids, pitiful arms. Still, as with Philippe Clay, such a horrific appearance only does more to bring out the sensitive soul inside.'"[8]

Still, Serge soldiered on, slogging through a divorce and the death of his close friend and ardent defender in the press, Boris Vian[9]. Looking back, Serge would call these early years his "blue period". It's not hard to discern why: the themes explored in his early, jazz-influenced – and later, latin-tinged – work are exceedingly dark and profoundly melancholy. On the subject of happiness, Serge proclaimed: *"I'm not capable of writing a happy, optimistic song, a love song. I can't find the words, I've nothing to say about happiness, I don't know what it is. It can't be expressed. It's as though you trained your camera lens on a perfectly blue sky. There would be nothing on the film. Whereas if you took a photograph of a stormy sky, with beautiful black and gray clouds, the effect would be stunning."*[10]

8 Gainsbourg, Verlant, **2000**, Albin Michel. Translation by Paul Knobloch.

9 Boris Vian (1920-1959) was a French novelist, poet, singer/songwriter, musician, and engineer. His 1947 novel *L'écume des jours* (*Froth on the Daydream*) has become a standard of French literature. For more on Vian, see the introductory notes to *Intoxicated Man* [1962].

10 Gainsbourg in Time, Verlant, **February 2001**, Gala Magazine.

LES AMOURS PERDUES — LOST LOVES [1954]

Signed Lucien Ginsburg (the singer's birth name), this was among the first songs Gainsbourg ever wrote. At the time, he was married to his first wife, Élisabeth Levitsky. The two would divorce in 1957. This was a few years after Serge, having decided to pursue a career in music rather than art, destroyed most of his own paintings.

The song is strikingly pessimistic, even by Gainsbourg's standards.

> Lost loves
> Are never to be found
> And jilted lovers
> May as well stop searching
>
> Lost loves
> Are never far, how-
> Ever, as jilted lovers
> Cannot forget
>
> **The vows of the heart**
> **The oaths of love**
> **The hold-me hold-me in your arms**
> **My love**
> **We will love each other**
> **Forever, Forever**
> **Forever, Forever**
> **Forever, For...**
>
> Lost loves
> Are never to be found
> And jilted lovers
> May as well stop searching
>
> My lost loves
> Always haunt my nights
> And to unknown arms
> I turn to forget them
>
> You, you'll love me
> I won't believe you[11]
> It will all end up like the days
> Of my first loves

---

11 The original lyrics use the future tense.

LES AMOURS PERDUES

Les amours perdues
Ne se retrouvent plus
Et les amants délaissés
Peuvent toujours chercher

Les amours perdues
Ne sont pas loin, pour-
Tant, car les amants délaissés
Ne peuvent oublier

Tous les serments de cœur
Tous les serments d'amour
Tous les serre-moi serre-moi dans tes bras
Mon amour
On s'aimera
Toujours, toujours
Toujours, toujours
Toujours, tou...

Les amours perdues
Ne se retrouvent plus
Et les amants délaissés
Peuvent toujours chercher

Mes amours perdues
Hantent toujours mes nuits
Et dans des bras inconnus
Je veux trouver l'oubli

Toi tu m'aimeras
Je ne te croirai pas
Tout reviendra comme au jour
De mes premières amours

Chorus

Lost loves
Are never to be found
And jilted lovers
May as well stop searching, searching, searching

Refrain

Les amours perdues
Ne se retrouvent plus
Et les amants délaissés
Peuvent toujours chercher, chercher, chercher

Paroles et musique Serge Gainsbourg

LE POINÇONNEUR DES LILAS — THE LILAS TICKET PUNCHER [1958]

This song has become the most popular of Gainsbourg's early works. The singer himself intimated that he wrote it after asking a ticket puncher what kept him going through a day's work; the ticket puncher purportedly replied: *"seeing the sky".***

Much later on, Gainsbourg would allege that the James Bond theme song borrowed heavily from the melody of his *Le poinçonneur des Lilas.* Incidentally, the man who composed the James Bond theme, John Barry, was Jane Birkin's[12] first husband.

One of the first Scopitone films (music video forerunners) featured Gainsbourg dressed as a ticket puncher in the Porte des Lilas station.

I'm the Lilas[13] ticket puncher
Briefly encountered and roundly ignored
There's no sun below ground
Not much of a cruise[14]
To kill time, I've in my vest
Condensed books from Reader's Digest

And in this book it's written
That some guys live the good life in Miami
While I'm stuck looking like a fool
Deep down in this cave
They say all work is noble
Me, I punch holes in tickets

I punch holes, little holes
More little holes
Little holes, little holes
Always little holes
Second class holes
First class holes

I punch holes, little holes
More little holes
Little holes, little holes
Always little holes
Little holes, little holes
Little holes, little holes

---

12 Jane Birkin (1946-) is a British actress and singer. For more on Birkin, who was the love of Gainsbourg's life, see the introductory notes to the section titled *Je T'aime Moi Non Plus: When Serge Meets Jane.*

13 Porte des Lilas is a station on lines 11 and 3bis of the Paris metro.

14 Gainsbourg compares the metro train to a cruise ship in this verse. This metaphor foreshadows the Miami reference in the next stanza.

LE POINÇONNEUR DES LILAS

J'suis l'poinçonneur des Lilas
Le gars qu'on croise et qu'on n'regarde pas
Y'a pas d'soleil sous la terre
Drôle de croisière
Pour tuer l'ennui, j'ai dans ma veste
Les extraits du "Reader's Digest"

Et dans c'bouquin y'a écrit
Que des gars s'la coulent douce à Miami
Pendant c'temps que je fais l'zouave
Au fond d'la cave
Paraît qu'y a pas d'sot métier
Moi j'fais des trous dans des billets

J'fais des trous, des p'tits trous
Encore des p'tits trous
Des p'tits trous, des p'tits trous
Toujours des p'tits trous
Des trous d'seconde classe
Des trous d'première classe

J'fais des trous, des p'tits trous
Encore des p'tits trous
Des p'tits trous, des p'tits trous
Toujours des p'tits trous
Des petits trous, des petits trous
Des petits trous, des petits trous

I'm the Lilas ticket puncher
For Invalides transfer at Opéra[15]
I live at the heart of the planet
I've in my head
A carnival of confetti
Some of which finds its way into my bed

And in my delftware[16] sky
I see only transfer lights glimmering[17]
At times I dream, I become delirious
I see waves
And in the fog at the end of the dock
I see a boat that's come to get me

To get me out of this hellhole
Where I punch holes
Little holes, little holes
Always little holes
But the boat's getting out of here
And I see myself becoming unglued

And so I remain in my hellhole
Punching little holes
Little holes, little holes
Always little holes
Little holes, little holes
Little holes, little holes

I'm the Lilas ticket puncher
For Arts et Métiers direct toward Levallois[18]
I'm tired, I've had it
With this cesspool
I'd like to disappear into thin air
And leave my cap in the changing room

---

15 Invalides and Opéra are both Paris metro stations.

16 Almost all Paris metro stations are tiled in white from floor to ceiling, with the station name standing out in navy blue. Gainsbourg used a more generic term ("porcelain") but "delftware" better conveys the night sky color scheme.

17 Your translator personally experienced the glimmering light phenomenon, as some Paris metro stations were still equipped with light-up navigation maps in the 2000's. The basic principle: press the button corresponding to the desired destination and an itinerary will light up on a large map, showing all transfers and stops along the way.

18 The Arts et Métiers stop is on both lines 11 and 3. The last stop on line 3 (westbound) is Pont de Levallois.

J'suis l'poinçonneur des Lilas
Pour Invalides changer à Opéra
Je vis au cœur d'la planète
J'ai dans la tête
Un carnaval de confettis
J'en amène jusque dans mon lit

Et sous mon ciel de faïence
Je n'vois briller que les correspondances
Parfois je rêve, je divague
Je vois des vagues
Et dans la brume au bout du quai
J'vois un bateau qui vient m'chercher

Pour m'sortir de ce trou
Où je fais des trous
Des p'tits trous, des p'tits trous
Toujours des p'tits trous
Mais l'bateau se taille
Et j'vois qu'je déraille

Et je reste dans mon trou
À faire des p'tits trous
Des p'tits trous, des p'tits trous
Toujours des p'tits trous
Des petits trous, des petits trous
Des petits trous, des petits trous

J'suis l'poinçonneur des Lilas
Arts et Métiers direct par Levallois
J'en ai marre, j'en ai ma claque
De ce cloaque
Je voudrais jouer la fille de l'air
Laisser ma casquette au vestiaire

A day will come I'm certain
When I'll be able to escape out into the world
I'll take off on the main road out of town
And I'll do whatever it takes
And if time runs out on me
I'll leave feet first

I punch holes, little holes
More little holes
Little holes, little holes
Always little holes
It's enough to drive one crazy
Enough to grab a gun

To make oneself a hole, a little hole
One last little hole
A little hole, a little hole
One last little hole
And I'll be placed in a big hole
And I won't hear any more talk of holes
Never again, no more holes, no more small holes
No more small holes, no more small holes

Un jour viendra j'en suis sûr
Où j'pourrai m'évader dans la nature
J'partirai sur la grand-route
Et coûte que coûte
Et si pour moi il est plus temps
Je partirai les pieds devant

J'fais des trous, des p'tits trous
Encore des p'tits trous
Des p'tits trous, des p'tits trous
Toujours des p'tits trous
Y'a d'quoi devenir dingue
De quoi prendre un flingue

S'faire un trou, un p'tit trou
Un dernier p'tit trou
Un p'tit trou, un p'tit trou
Un dernier p'tit trou
Et on m'mettra dans un grand trou
Et j'n'entendrai plus parler d'trous
Plus jamais d'trous, de petits trous
De petits trous, de petits trous

Paroles et musique de Serge Gainsbourg
© Warner Chappell Music France/Melody Nelson Publishing

CE MORTEL ENNUI — THIS DEADLY BOREDOM [1958]

Gainsbourg firmly establishes his misogynistic reputation with this dark and provocative song.

This deadly boredom
That hits me
When I am
With you
This deadly boredom
That latches on to me
And matches my
Every step

The day when I'll be
Over you and have enough guts
To leave you
That day, oh! yes
That day I think, yes
I think I will be able to see
This deadly boredom beat
A retreat far away from me

Of course nothing needs to be said
Horizontally
But we no longer have anything to say to each other
Vertically
So to kill time between lovemaking
And lovemaking
I grab the paper and my pen
And shade in the A's and the O's[19]

One day I'll end up having to decide
My love
To pack my bags
But I'm afraid you'll go to the bathroom
And reach for
The barbiturates

Since I don't want
Any problems with
My conscience and your father
I let it go on

---

19 The vowels "a" and "o" are precisely the ones Serge added to his last name to change it from Ginsburg to Gainsbourg.**

CE MORTEL ENNUI

Ce mortel ennui
Qui me vient
Quand je suis
Avec toi
Ce mortel ennui
Qui me tient
Et me suit
Pas à pas

Le jour où j'aurai assez
D'estomac et de toi
Pour te laisser choir
Ce jour-là, oh ! oui
Ce jour-là je crois, oui
Je crois que je pourrai voir
Ce mortel ennui se tailler
À l'anglaise loin de moi

Bien sûr il n'est rien besoin de dire
À l'horizontale
Mais on ne trouve plus rien à se dire
À la verticale
Alors pour tuer le temps entre l'amour
Et l'amour
J'prends l'journal et mon stylo
Et je remplis et les A et les O

Il faudra bien que j'me décide un jour
Mon amour
À me faire la malle
Mais j'ai peur qu'tu n'ailles dans la salle de bains
Tendre la main
Vers le gardénal

Comme j'veux pas
D'ennui avec ma
Conscience et ton père
Je m'laisse faire

Paroles et musique Serge Gainsbourg
© Warner Chappell Music France/Melody Nelson Publishing

DU JAZZ DANS LE RAVIN — RAVINE JAZZ [1958]

Gainsbourg probably drew inspiration for this song from the serious accident Françoise Sagan[20] suffered in 1957 while driving an Aston Martin.* Sagan, a self-described speed addict, would often drive her Jaguar to Monte Carlo for gambling sessions.

When the narrator appears in the third stanza, his phlegmatic delivery is reminiscent of Nick Carraway's own detachment after coming across a similar (yet non-fatal) accident following one of Gatsby's lavish parties.

> Listen[21] are you driving or am I
> I am, right well then shut up
> There's whiskey in the glovebox
> And Camels[22] you might as well help yourself
>
> Listen, listen here babe
> You hear my favorite tune
> Turn up the radio a bit for me
> And don't be scared, I won't crash
>
> Suddenly just before Monte Carlo
> That's it, that's bad luck for you
> The Jaguar went and lurched wildly
> And ended up straight ahead in that ditch
>
> And while both of 'em lay there dying
> The radio, the radio kept on blaring
> Tomorrow they'll come scrape them off the road

---

20 Françoise Sagan (1935-2004) was a French novelist, playwright and screenwriter. She wrote her best-known novel, *Bonjour Tristesse*, when she was a teenager.

21 "Listen" is also used as an opener in *L'eau à la bouche* [1960] and *Requiem pour un con* [1968].

22 Gainsbourg uses the term "américaines", which could have referred to any American brand of cigarettes sold in France at the time.

DU JAZZ DANS LE RAVIN

Écoute c'est toi qui conduis ou moi
C'est moi, bon alors tais-toi
Y'a du whisky dans la boîte à gants
Et des américaines t'as qu'à taper dedans

Écoute, écoute un peu ça poupée
T'entends mon air préféré
Mets-moi la radio un peu plus fort
Et n'aie pas peur, j'vais pas aller dans les décors

Soudain juste avant Monte-Carlo
C'est ça, c'est ça l'manque de pot
V'là qu'la Jaguar fait une embardée
Et droit devant la v'là qui pique dans le fossé

Et pendant qu'tous deux agonisaient
La radio, la radio a continué d'gueuler
Demain on les ramassera à la p'tite cuillère

Paroles et musique Serge Gainsbourg
© Warner Chappell Music France/Melody Nelson Publishing

LE CLAQUEUR DE DOIGTS — I SNAP MY FINGERS [1959]

This is the first track off Serge's second album, unpretentiously titled *Serge Gainsbourg nº2*. Notes of American rock and roll permeate the piece, which constitutes a departure from the jazzy style of the first album and is a sign of things to come. Serge even goes so far as to include a rather trite reference to blue jeans.

On first listen, your translator was immediately reminded of Ray Charles' *Hit The Road Jack*. It turns out that the earliest version of Charles' song, an *a cappella* ditty recorded by Percy Mayfield, was released in 1960. Might Mayfield have been inspired by Gainsbourg?

Jukebox, jukebox
I snap my fingers in front of the jukebox
Jukebox, jukebox
I snap my fingers in front of the jukebox

Chorus

When I'm not running them all over you
I don't know what to do with my ten fingers
I don't know what to do with my ten fingers
So I snap them
Snap, snap, snap
In front of the

Chorus x3

I still have for the machine
Plenty of change in my blue jeans
Plenty of change in my blue jeans
I have to slap
Slap, slap, slap
It in the slot

Chorus x3

Oh! Sylvie[23], look at me
Who's this guy hitting on you
Who's this guy hitting on you
He's gonna make me snap
Snap, snap, snap
In front of the

---

23 Sylvie Rivet was a press officer for Philips, which put out the majority of Serge's albums throughout his career. In 1959, Gainsbourg went on tour and purportedly had a liaison with Ms. Rivet,* who would later go on to live with Jacques Brel between 1960 and 1970.

LE CLAQUEUR DE DOIGTS

Juke-box, juke-box
J'suis claqueur de doigts devant les juke-box
Juke-box, juke-box
Je claque des doigts devant les juke-box

Refrain

Quand ils n's'baladent pas sur toi
Je n'sais qu'faire de mes dix doigts
Je n'sais qu'faire de mes dix doigts
Alors j'les claque
Claque, claque, claque
Devant les

Refrain trissé

J'ai encore pour la machine
D'la mitraille dans mes blue-jeans
D'la mitraille dans mes blue-jeans
Faut que j'la claque
Claque, claque, claque
Dedans le

Refrain trissé

Oh ! Sylvie, regarde-moi
Qui est c'type qui t'fait du plat
Qui est c'type qui t'fait du plat
J'en ai ma claque
Claque, claque, claque
De ce gars

Jukebox, jukebox
If he ever comes over by the jukebox
Jukebox, jukebox
I'll snap his head off in front of the jukebox

Juke-box, juke-box
Si jamais il s'approche du juke-box
Juke-box, juke-box
J'lui claquerai la gueule devant le juke-box

Paroles et musique Serge Gainsbourg

INDIFFÉRENTE — INDIFFERENT[24] [1959]

This song finds Gainsbourg indulging in a diatribe against a woman's perceived frigidity. It is also home to one of his most cutting couplets: "In your eyes I see mine, you're so lucky / A glimmer of intelligence now inhabits you".

Like that dog Jean de Nivelle[25]
You never come when I call

What does time matter
The wind sweeps it away
I'll take your absence
Over your irrelevance

When by chance I find you in my bed
It's never clear if you're consenting or not

What does time matter
The wind sweeps it away
I'll take your absence
Over your insolence

In your eyes I see mine, you're so lucky
A glimmer of intelligence now inhabits you

What does time matter
The wind sweeps it away
I'll take your absence
Over your incoherence

In different circumstances, I would sing the praises
Of love, but these days I don't give a damn

What does time matter
The wind sweeps it away
I'll take your absence
Over your indifference

---

24 The French adjective is in the feminine form (indifférente).

25 Jean de Nivelle (1422-1467) was disinherited by his father when he refused to fight for King Louis XI and instead took the Duke of Burgundy's side in what would eventually become the Mad War (1485-1488). Legend has it that the people then gave Jean the insulting nickname "chien de Jean de Nivelle", or "that dog Jean de Nivelle".

INDIFFÉRENTE

Comme le chien de monsieur Jean de Nivelle
Tu ne viens jamais à moi quand je t'appelle

Qu'importe le temps
Qu'emporte le vent
Mieux vaut ton absence
Que ton inconséquence

Quand par hasard dans mon lit je te rencontre
On n'peut pas dire qu'tu sois pour ni qu'tu sois contre

Qu'importe le temps
Qu'emporte le vent
Mieux vaut ton absence
Que ton impertinence

Dans tes yeux je vois mes yeux, t'en as d'la chance
Ça te donne des lueurs d'intelligence

Qu'importe le temps
Qu'emporte le vent
Mieux vaut ton absence
Que ton incohérence

En d'autre occasion, je chanterai les transes
De l'amour, mais aujourd'hui je m'en balance

Qu'importe le temps
Qu'emporte le vent
Mieux vaut ton absence
Que ton indifférence

Paroles Serge Gainsbourg
Musique Alain Goraguer
© Warner Chappell Music France/Melody Nelson Publishing

L'EAU À LA BOUCHE — WHEN MY MOUTH WATERS [1960]

Gainsbourg's first big hit. It was written for a film of the same title by Jacques Doniol-Valcroze, a little-known *nouvelle vague* director.*

Listen to my voice, listen to my prayer
Listen to my heartbeat, don't resist
I beg you, don't be unyielding
When my mouth waters

I want you confident, yet you seem captive
I want you docile, yet you seem fearful
I beg you, don't be unyielding
When my mouth waters

Let the current take you
To the river's bed
And to mine
If you please
Let's leave the riverbank
Let's drift away

I will take you gently and without coercion
What are you afraid of, come now, have no fear
I beg you, don't be unyielding
When my mouth waters

Tonight, you'll come lie close to me
Yes, I will be gentle, I will wait for you
And so as not to scare you off
Look... I'm only taking your mouth

L'EAU À LA BOUCHE

Écoute ma voix, écoute ma prière
Écoute mon cœur qui bat, laisse-toi faire
Je t'en prie, ne sois pas farouche
Quand me vient l'eau à la bouche

Je te veux confiante, je te sens captive
Je te veux docile, je te sens craintive
Je t'en prie, ne sois pas farouche
Quand me vient l'eau à la bouche

Laisse-toi au gré du courant
Porter dans le lit du torrent
Et dans le mien
Si tu veux bien
Quittons la rive
Partons à la dérive

Je te prendrai doucement et sans contrainte
De quoi as-tu peur, allons, n'aie nulle crainte
Je t'en prie, ne sois pas farouche
Quand me vient l'eau à la bouche

Cette nuit, près de moi, tu viendras t'étendre
Oui, je serai calme, je saurai t'attendre
Et pour que tu ne t'effarouches
Vois… Je ne prends que ta bouche

Paroles Serge Gainsbourg
Musique Serge Gainsbourg et Alain Goraguer
© Warner Chappell Music France/Melody Nelson Publishing

LA CHANSON DE PRÉVERT — PRÉVERT'S SONG [1960]

This song is a tribute to *Les feuilles mortes*, a poem penned by Jacques Prévert[26] in 1945 and subsequently set to music by Joseph Kosma[27].

The English version of the song – titled *Autumn Leaves* and translated by Johnny Mercer - was popularized by a number of well-known artists, including Nat King Cole, Jo Stafford, and Roger Williams. In 1955, Williams' version reached #1 single status in Billboard Magazine's rankings. It remains the only piano instrumental to have achieved that rank to date.

"Oh how I would like for you to remember"[28]
This was your song
It was your favorite
I think
It is by Prévert and
Kosma

And the autumn leaves never fail
To bring you back to mind
Day after day, lost loves
Never cease to be lost[29]

To others of course, I give myself
But their song is monotone
And little by little I grow indif-
Ferent
There is nothing to be done
About it

Because the autumn leaves never fail
To bring you back to mind
Day after day, lost loves
Never cease to be lost

---

26   Jacques Prévert (1900-1977) was a famous French poet and screenwriter.

27   Joseph Kosma (born József Kozma, 1905-1969) was a French-Hungarian composer who immigrated to France from Germany in 1933 after having studied under Béla Bartók at Budapest's famed Ferenc Liszt Music Academy.

28   Gainsbourg lifted his opening line from Prévert's poem.

29   The French version is significantly more morbid. Literally translated, the leaves would be "dead", and "dead loves" would "never cease to die".
Note: the French word for love, "amour", is a masculine noun. However, Gainsbourg feminizes it by following it with the feminine form of the adjective "dead" ("mortes"). One can argue that this is poetic license to maintain the rhyme with "feuilles mortes" ("feuille" being a feminine noun). Or perhaps love transcends grammar.

LA CHANSON DE PRÉVERT

"Oh ! je voudrais tant que tu te souviennes"
Cette chanson était la tienne
C'était ta préférée
Je crois
Qu'elle est de Prévert et
Kosma

Et chaque fois "Les feuilles mortes"
Te rappellent à mon souvenir
Jour après jour, les amours mortes
N'en finissent pas de mourir

Avec d'autres bien sûr, je m'abandonne
Mais leur chanson est monotone
Et peu à peu je m'in-
Diffère
À cela il n'est rien
À faire

Car chaque fois "Les feuilles mortes"
Te rappellent à mon souvenir
Jour après jour, les amours mortes
N'en finissent pas de mourir

Will we never know where indifference
Begins and when it ends
May autumn give way
To winter
And may Prévert's
Song

That song "Autumn Leaves"
Be erased from my memory
And on that day, my lost loves
Will cease to be lost
And on that day, my lost loves
Will cease to be lost

Peut-on jamais savoir par où commence
Et quand finit l'indifférence
Passe l'automne, vienne
L'hiver
Et que la chanson de
Prévert

Cette chanson, "Les feuilles mortes"
S'efface de mon souvenir
Et ce jour-là, mes amours mortes
En auront fini de mourir
Et ce jour-là, mes amours mortes
En auront fini de mourir

Paroles et musique Serge Gainsbourg
© Warner Chappell Music France/Melody Nelson Publishing

BLACK TROMBONE [1962]

A loving tribute to jazz, this song is less about the lyrics and more about the music. The backstory, with sensuality and a touch of misogyny, recounts a tale of female conquest before closing with a healthy dose of pessimism.

Black trombone
Monotone
Trombone
Sounds nice
Swirls around
Gramophone
And muzzles
My boredom

Black trombone
Monotone
Native son
Of the night
God forgive
The cute girl
Humming along
In my bed

Black trombone
Monotone
She offers herself up
Half-naked
Shivering
I'm losing it
She's poisoning me
She's invading me

Black trombone
Monotone
It's the autumn
Of my life
Nobody surprises
Me anymore
I give up
It's over

BLACK TROMBONE

Black trombone
Monotone
Le trombone
C'est joli
Tourbillonne
Gramophone
Et bâillonne
Mon ennui

Black trombone
Monotone
Autochtone
De la nuit
Dieu pardonne
La mignonne
Qui fredonne
Dans mon lit

Black trombone
Monotone
Elle se donne
À demi
Nue, frissonne
Déraisonne
M'empoisonne
M'envahit

Black trombone
Monotone
C'est l'automne
De ma vie
Plus personne
Ne m'étonne
J'abandonne
C'est fini

INTOXICATED MAN [1962]

This song reeks of alcohol, one of Gainsbourg's most public vices. The first couplet is lifted from Boris Vian's[30] song *Je bois* [1955]. The musical style of the song is also an homage to Vian, who was an erudite connoisseur of American jazz. Gainsbourg and Vian quickly became fast friends, and the latter was an early inspiration for the former. Not only did Vian's uninhibited onstage antics persuade Gainsbourg to try his hand at singing, but the author even helped launch his friend's career with a glowing review of Serge's first album in the satirical-but-informed weekly *Le canard enchaîné.*[31]

In June of 1959, Vian attended the premiere of the film adaptation of his sado-erotic crime novel *J'irai cracher sur vos tombes* (*I'll Spit on Your Graves*). He had been critical throughout the film-making process, even requesting that his name be struck from the credits. Minutes into the screening, Vian stood up and shouted his disapproval before collapsing in his seat. At thirty-nine years of age, he died of cardiac arrest en route to the hospital.

> I drink
> Too heavily
> I see
> Pink elephants
> Spiders on the lapel
> Of my tuxedo
> Bats on the ceiling
> Of the living-
> Room
>
> **Hey! you**
> **Tell me something**
> **You stand there**
> **Like a pink marble statue**
> **Stiff**[32] **as the lapel**
> **Of my tuxedo**
> **Pale as the ceiling**
> **Of the living-**
> **Room**

---

30   Boris Vian (1920-1959) was a French novelist, poet, singer/songwriter, musician, and engineer. His 1947 novel *L'écume des jours* (*Froth on the Daydream*) has become a standard of French literature.

31   The article, which was included in the issue published on November 12th, 1958, can be found in Chapter 5 of Gilles Verlant's biography: Gainsbourg, Verlant, **2000**, Albin Michel. Translation by Paul Knobloch.

32   After *Indifférente* [1959], the theme of frigidity makes another appearance: the French lyrics ("glacée") leave no doubt as to the sex of the singer's mute interlocutor.

INTOXICATED MAN

Je bois
À trop forte dose
Je vois
Des éléphants roses
Des araignées sur le plastron
D'mon smoking
Des chauves-souris au plafond
Du living-
Room

Eh ! toi
Dis-moi quelque chose
Tu es là
Comme un marbre rose
Aussi glacée que le plastron
D'mon smoking
Aussi pâle que le plafond
Du living-
Room

Love
No longer interests me much
I still see
Those pink elephants
Those spiders on the lapel
Of my tuxedo
Those bats on the ceiling
Of the living-
Room

Chorus

L'amour
Me dit plus grand-chose
Toujours
Ces éléphants roses
Ces araignées sur le plastron
D'mon smoking
Ces chauves-souris au plafond
Du living-
Room

Refrain

Paroles et musique Serge Gainsbourg
© Warner Chappell Music France / Melody Nelson Publishing

QUAND TU T'Y METS — WHEN YOU THROW YOURSELF INTO IT [1962]

Pointed lyrics are set to an intoxicating, trumpet-led jazz beat complete with two bass lines, one acoustic and the other electric. The bass line quite resembles the one featured in Peggy Lee's rendition of Little Willie John's 1956 hit *Fever*.

How pretty you can be when you throw yourself into it
You don't often throw yourself into it
But when you do throw yourself into it
If you only knew

How bitchy you can be when you throw yourself into it
You don't often throw yourself into it
But when you do throw yourself into it
If you only knew

How much you can hurt me when you throw yourself into it
You don't often throw yourself into it
But when you do throw yourself into it
If you only knew

How you land in my arms when you throw yourself into them
You rarely throw yourself into them anymore
But when you do throw yourself into them
If you only knew

How lovely our love was when we were in love
And yet 'twas not so long ago
That we were in love
If you only remembered

QUAND TU T'Y METS

C'que tu peux être belle quand tu t'y mets
Tu t'y mets pas souvent
Pourtant quand tu t'y mets
Tu peux pas savoir

C'que tu peux être garce quand tu t'y mets
Tu t'y mets pas souvent
Pourtant quand tu t'y mets
Tu peux pas savoir

C'que tu peux m'faire mal quand tu t'y mets
Tu t'y mets pas souvent
Pourtant quand tu t'y mets
Tu peux pas savoir

C'que tu es dans mes bras quand tu t'y mets
Tu t'y mets plus souvent
Pourtant quand tu t'y mets
Tu peux pas savoir

C'qu'était notre amour quand on s'aimait
Il n'y'a pas si longtemps
Pourtant que l'on s'aimait
Tu dois plus savoir

Paroles et musique Serge Gainsbourg
© Warner Chappell Music France/Melody Nelson Publishing

LES CIGARILLOS — CIGARILLOS [1962]

Les cigarillos is to tobacco what *Intoxicated man* was to liquor. Gainsbourg was known to smoke three packs a day of *Gitanes* (see 1980's *Dieu fumeur de havanes*) and thousands of photographs show him in the act.

Gainsbourg vaunts the merits of tobacco as a confidence aide when it comes to wooing women, but makes no attempt to gloss over the fleeting quality of his conquests' attachment. Due in part to incessant criticism of his rough-hewn and atypical looks, Gainsbourg struggled mightily with his self-esteem throughout his life.

The upside to cigarillos is that they police my personal space
Their tobacco is lovely
As is their thoughtfulness
Cigarillos, unlike me, are not steeped in diffidence
And their aggressiveness
Is quite nuanced
With nary a hurtful word
They politely usher you to the door

Ah! lovely tobacco, lovely tobacco[33]
Lovely tobacco, lovely tobacco
Ah! lovely tobacco, lovely tobacco
Lovely tobacco, lovely tobacco

Cigarillos often elicit tearful goodbyes
From mistresses
And courtesans
The cigarillos know as well as I do that they mourn not
My handsome eyes, but rather
The end of the cuban
Without waiting for full consummation
They all disappear into the mist

Chorus x2

Ah! lovely tobacco, lovely tobacco
Lovely tobacco, lovely tobacco

---

33 In French, "faire un tabac" (literally, "to make tobacco") is an expression that means "to enjoy success". By extension and in context, "quel tabac" ("what [lovely] tobacco") can be taken to mean "what success [these cigarillos allow me to have with women]". Unfortunately, this play on words is untranslatable.

LES CIGARILLOS

Les cigarillos ont cet avantage de faire le vide autour de moi
J'en apprécie le tabac
Et la prévenance
Les cigarillos n'sont pas comme moi empreints de timidité
Et leur agressivité
Est toute en nuance
Sans vous dire jamais rien qui vous blesse
Ils vous congédient avec tendresse

Ah ! quel tabac, quel tabac
Quel tabac, quel tabac
Ah ! quel tabac, quel tabac
Quel tabac, quel tabac

Les cigarillos me valent bien souvent les adieux éplorés
Des femmes de qualité
Et des courtisanes
Les cigarillos savent comme moi que ce n'sont pas mes beaux yeux
Qu'elles implorent, mais un peu
La fin du havane
Sans attendre que tout se consume
Elles disparaissent dans la brume

Refrain bissé

Ah ! quel tabac, quel tabac
Quel tabac, quel tabac

Paroles et musique Serge Gainsbourg
© Warner Chappell Music France/Melody Nelson Publishing

REQUIEM POUR UN TWISTEUR — REQUIEM FOR A TWIST DANCER [1962]

Gainsbourg's first requiem (*Requiem pour un con* would follow five years later) finds him sardonically foreshadowing the death of the twist craze, which was at its peak in the early 1960's. Gainsbourg detachedly inflicts cardiac arrest on the hapless Charlie to end the song. Incidentally, Gainsbourg also died of a heart attack — see introductory notes to the final chapter of this book.

Tell me have you ever met Charlie
Had you not I would have been surprised
There's not a club he didn't go to
What a party animal

Requiem for a twist dancer

Tell me have you ever seen him drunk
Had you not I would have been surprised
There's not a night he wasn't tight
What a clown

Requiem for a twist dancer

Tell me were you in love with him
Were you not I would have been surprised
There's not a woman who withstood his charm
What a lady-killer

Requiem for a twist dancer
Requiem for a twist dancer
Requiem for a twist dancer

Tell me did all that last long
Had it I would have been surprised
Personally I think his heart gave way
How terrible

Requiem for a twist dancer
Requiem for a twist dancer
Requiem for a twist dancer

REQUIEM POUR UN TWISTEUR

Dites-moi avez-vous connu Charlie
Le contraire m'eût étonné
Il n'est pas une boîte qu'il n'ait fréquentée
Quel noceur

Requiem pour un twisteur

Dites-moi l'avez-vous connu à jeun
Le contraire m'eût étonné
Il n'est pas un soir qu'il ne fût bourré
Quel farceur

Requiem pour un twisteur

Dites-moi étiez-vous amoureuse de lui
Le contraire m'eût étonné
Il n'est pas une femme qui lui ait résisté
Quel tombeur

Requiem pour un twisteur
Requiem pour un twisteur
Requiem pour un twisteur

Dites-moi tout ça n'pouvait pas durer
Le contraire m'eût étonné
Je crois quant à moi qu'c'est l'cœur qui a lâché
Quelle horreur

Requiem pour un twisteur
Requiem pour un twisteur
Requiem pour un twisteur

Paroles et musique Serge Gainsbourg
© Warner Chappell Music France/Melody Nelson Publishing

LA JAVANAISE [1963]

In the summer of 1962, Gainsbourg and Juliette Gréco, the famous singer/actress, spent an evening together at Gréco's residence in Paris on the rue de Verneuil (Serge later bought his own home on the same street in 1968). They listened to classical music and drank fine wine; Gréco even improvised a dance (probably dubbed "la javanaise" by the two friends). The next morning, Gainsbourg had orchids delivered to Gréco's door, along with lyrics to a song that would become a timeless classic.*

Javanais is an obsolete form of French pig-latin in which the syllables *ja* or *av* were inserted into words so as to render conversations unintelligible to the passing novice.* Gainsbourg uses liberal doses of these two syllables in his lyrics.

Every effort was made to infuse this translation with the elegant, syncopated rhythm of the original work.

It's true
I had
Struggled
Not you
My love
Before
Having
Heard tell
Of you
My love

I mean no offense but
While dancing the javanaise
We were in love
At least for a song's time

What do
You think
What do
We know
Of love
From me
To you
You got
Me good
My love

Chorus

Alas
April
In vain

LA JAVANAISE

J'avoue
J'en ai
Bavé
Pas vous
Mon amour
Avant
D'avoir
Eu vent
De vous
Mon amour

Ne vous déplaise
En dansant la javanaise
Nous nous aimions
Le temps d'une chanson

À votre
Avis
Qu'avons-
Nous vu
De l'amour
De vous
À moi
Vous m'a-
Vez eu
Mon amour

Refrain

Hélas
Avril
En vain

Binds me
To love
I wan-
Ted so
To see
In you
This love

Chorus

This life's
Not worth
Living
Without love
But it's
You who
Wanted
It so
My love

Chorus

Me voue
À l'amour
J'avais
Envie
De voir
En vous
Cet amour

Refrain

La vie
Ne vaut
D'être
Vécue
Sans amour
Mais c'est
Vous qui
L'avez
Voulu
Mon amour

Refrain

Paroles et musique de Serge Gainsbourg

CHEZ LES YÉ-YÉ — A NIGHT WITH THE YÉ-YÉ'S [1963]

The narrator is on a mission to save a Lolita held captive by a group of yé-yé's (see introductory notes to the *Yé-Yé Mania* chapter for further context).

Gainsbourg plays off the name of the Yé-Yé movement in the lyrics by inserting numerous words containing repetitions of the same syllable or sound.

Neither the yé-yé tam-tams
Nor the gri-gris[34] that you wore
Nor the "da doo ron ron"[35] that you listened to
At the ball[36] where you danced

No, nothing will stop me
I'll come find you my Lolita[37]
Among the
Yé-yé

To the beat of the yé-yé tam-tams
I'll make a ruckus I know myself
I'll end up in Sing-Sing[38]
I've got a switch-switch blade

No, nothing will stop me
I'll come find you my Lolita
Among the
Yé-yé

To the beat of the yé-yé tam-tams
Flash back to the past
Can you hear what I was saying to you
I'm cra-, cra-, crazy about you

---

34 A gri-gri is an African amulet believed to protect the wearer from evil or bad luck.

35 Reference to The Crystals' 1963 hit *Da Doo Ron Ron*.**

36 The original lyrics reference a "bal doum-doum" (the French word "bal" meaning "dancing ball"). This is a subtle play on words: the term "dum-dum bullet" - designating a particular type of bullet meant to fragment and cause maximum damage on impact - would be translated to French as "balle doum-doum" ("balle", pronounced the same way as "bal", means "bullet", and "doum-doum" is a phonetic interpretation of "dum-dum"). This play on words perpetuates the syllable repetition theme (with "doum-doum"). Unfortunately, it is quite untranslatable.

37 First appearance of the term "Lolita" in Gainsbourg's lyrics. Nabokov's novel *Lolita* was translated to French in 1959.*

38 The famous New York state prison is referenced here.

CHEZ LES YÉ-YÉ

Ni les tam-tams du yé-yé-yé-é
Ni les gris-gris que tu portais
"Da doo ron ron" que tu écoutais
Au bal doum-doum où tu dansais

Non, rien n'aura raison de moi
J'irai t'chercher ma Lolita
Chez les
Yé-yé

Sous les tam-tams des yé-yé-yé-é
J'ferai du ramdam je me connais
Oui à Sing-Sing je finirai
J'ai un coupe-coupe à cran d'arrêt

Non, rien n'aura raison de moi
J'irai t'chercher ma Lolita
Chez les
Yé-yé

Sous les tam-tams des yé-yé-yé-é
Fais un flash-back au temps passé
Est-ce que t'entends c'que j'te disais
Je suis fou, fou, fou de t'aimer

But nothing will stop me
I'll come find you my Lolita
Among the
Yé-yé

Neither the yé-yé tam-tams
Nor the gri-gris that you wore
Nor the "da doo ron ron" that you listened to
At the ball where you danced

No, nothing will stop me
I'll come find you my Lolita
Among the
Yé-yé

To the beat of the yé-yé tam-tams
I'll make a ruckus I know myself
I'll end up at Sing-Sing
I've got a switch-switch blade

No, nothing will stop me
I'll come find you my Lolita
Among the
Yé-yé

To the beat of the yé-yé tam-tams
Flash back to the past
Can you hear what I was saying to you
I'm cra-, cra-, crazy about you

But nothing will stop me
I'll come find you my Lolita
Among the
Yé-yé

Neither the yé-yé tam-tams
Nor the gri-gris... *OK, that's enough!*

Mais rien n'aura raison de moi
J'irai t'chercher ma Lolita
Chez les
Yé-yé

Ni les tam-tams du yé-yé-yé-é
Ni les gris-gris que tu portais
"Da doo ron ron" que tu écoutais
Au bal doum-doum où tu dansais

Non, rien n'aura raison de moi
J'irai t'chercher ma Lolita
Chez les
Yé-yé

Sous les tam-tams des yé-yé-yé-é
J'ferai du ramdam je me connais
Oui à Sing-Sing je finirai
J'ai un coupe-coupe à cran d'arrêt

Non, rien n'aura raison de moi
J'irai t'chercher ma Lolita
Chez les
Yé-yé

Sous les tam-tams des yé-yé-yé-é
Fais un flash-back au temps passé
Est-ce que t'entends c'que j'te disais
Je suis fou, fou, fou de t'aimer

Mais rien n'aura raison de moi
J'irai t'chercher ma Lolita
Chez les
Yé-yé

Ni les tam-tams des yé-yé-yé-é
Ni les gris-gris... *Ouais, bon !*

Paroles et musique Serge Gainsbourg

LE TALKIE-WALKIE — THE WALKIE-TALKIE [1963]

This delightfully anachronistic song explores the theme of long-distance rejection.

I had in my possession a walkie-talkie
Made in Japan
At present what I'm left with is a touch of madness
Nothing else

I had given the same device to the one I loved
We called each other on impulse
Whether she was in her room
Or on the playground at school[39]
I could reach her whenever
Wherever

When I heard her voice in the walkie-talkie
I was happy
Until the day she forgot it by her bed
Here's how

I was alone with myself when I decided to call her
Right away I knew I was in for anguish
I don't wish a similar mo-
Ment on anyone
Long story short
Here's what happened

I heard sighs in the walkie-talkie
Sweet nothings
And then her name murmured into the night by
A stranger, from that day on

All of the fuses in my poor box were blown
But I see her in my darkness
I see her beige doe eyes
Both the color of time
Whence snow
Fell from time to time

I had in my possession a walkie-talkie
Made in Japan
At present what I'm left with is a touch of madness
Nothing else

---

39 By using the term "lycée", the original lyrics make it clear that the girl in question is at least a sophomore and at most a senior in high school.

LE TALKIE-WALKIE

J'avais en ma possession un talkie-walkie
Made in Japan
Il ne m'en reste à présent qu'un grain de folie
Un point c'est tout

J'avais donné le même appareil à celle que j'aimais
On s'appelait pour un oui, pour un non
Qu'elle soit dans sa cham-
Bre ou bien dans la cour de son lycée
Je l'avais n'importe quand
N'importe où

Quand j'entendais sa voix dans le talkie-walkie
J'étais heureux
Jusqu'au jour où elle l'oublia près de son lit
Voici comment

J'étais seul avec moi quand je décidai de l'appeler
J'ai tout de suite compris ma douleur
Je ne souhaite à perso-
Nne de vivre un moment pareil
En deux mots
Voilà ce qui s'est passé

J'entendis des soupirs dans le talkie-walkie
Des mots d'amour
Et puis son prénom que murmurait dans la nuit
Un inconnu, de ce jour

Tous les plombs de mon pauvre compteur ont sauté
Mais je la vois dans mon obscurité
Je vois ses grands yeux beiges
Ses deux grands yeux couleur du temps
D'où la neige
Tombait de temps en temps

J'avais en ma possession un talkie-walkie
Made in Japan
Il ne m'en reste à présent qu'un grain de folie
Un point c'est tout

Paroles et musique Serge Gainsbourg

LA SAISON DES PLUIES — THE RAINY SEASON [1963]

A lovely amalgam of gloomy weather and lost love.

This song first saw the light as an instrumental composed and recorded in early 1963 by Elek Bacsik, a Hungarian guitarist who had moved to Paris in 1959.*

Lyrics were soon added to the music by Jackie Lawrence.[40] Gainsbourg made a few edits to create a "male version", which he first recorded in December 1963, with Bacsik on the electric guitar.**

The translation offered below is of Gainsbourg's version.

> The rainy season is upon us
> Farewell to love stories
> I sit under the veranda and take in
> The tears of the girl I loved so[41]
>
> The rainy season is upon us
> Lovers bid farewell
> The sky is ashen, the air is moist
> More tears are on the horizon
>
> The air is becoming ever heavier
> And the weather ever more hostile
> The advent of the gloomy season
> Was inevitable
>
> The rainy season is upon us
> Farewell to love stories
> I got up from under the veranda and walked
> Toward the one I had loved so
>
> The rainy season is upon us
> Lovers bid farewell
> The mascara[42] at the corner of her mouth
> Will be erased by a newcomer's kiss

---

40 Jackie Lawrence was a French singer active in the 1950's and 1960's. Her work has largely been forgotten.

41 An example of the slight modifications made by Gainsbourg to Lawrence's lyrics: this line originally read "The tears of the man who loved me so".

42 The term used in the original lyrics is "rimmel". In French, this term used to be to mascara what "kleenex" is still to tissues in English.

LA SAISON DES PLUIES

C'est la saison des pluies
La fin des amours
Assis sous la véranda je regarde pleurer
Cette enfant que j'ai tant aimée

C'est la saison des pluies
L'adieu des amants
Le ciel est de plomb, il y'a d'l'humidité dans l'air
D'autres larmes en perspective

Le temps était de plus en plus lourd
Et le climat plus hostile
Il fallait bien que vienne enfin
La saison maussade

C'est la saison des pluies
La fin des amours
J'ai quitté la véranda et me suis approché
De celle que j'ai tant aimée

C'est la saison des pluies
L'adieu des amants
Un autre viendra qui d'un baiser effacera
Le rimmel au coin de ses lèvres

Paroles Serge Gainsbourg
Musique Elek Bacsik
© Melody Nelson Publishing & DR

SCENIC RAILWAY [1963]

The Scenic Railway is a wooden rollercoaster located at the site of the former Dreamland Amusement Park in Margate, England. The ride opened to the public in 1920 and is the oldest rollercoaster in the UK.

Could Gainsbourg have been complaining about a female partner's insistence on using pleasure-enhancing sex toys?

> Yeah, I'll take you
> On the Scenic Railway
> If that's what you want
> That's easy
>
> Yeah, I'll take you
> On the Scenic Railway
> We'll go tomorrow
> I promise
>
> **But don't you feel**
> **A tad simpleminded**
> **Will you ever understand**
> **All that love means**
>
> Yeah, I'll take you
> On the Scenic Railway
> That's all you're thinking about
> It's pathetic
>
> Yeah, I'll take you
> On the Scenic Railway
> But those thrills
> Are easy
>
> Yeah, I'll take you
> On the Scenic Railway
> So stop sulking
> I've agreed
>
> **Once on it you'll be**
> **Where I want you, my cruel girl**
> **Clinging to my arm**
> **The one bloodied by your nails**
>
> Yeah, I'm going to sound
> A bit cynical, yeah yeah
> Machines aren't the only way
> To get off

SCENIC RAILWAY

Ouais, je t'emmènerai
Sur le Scenic Railway
Si c'est ce que tu veux
C'est facile

Ouais, je t'emmènerai
Sur le Scenic Railway
On verra ça demain
C'est promis

Mais ne te sens-tu pas
Quelque peu inconsciente
Tout ce qu'aimer veut dire
Le sauras-tu un jour

Ouais, je t'emmènerai
Sur le Scenic Railway
Tu n'as que ça en tête
C'est terrible

Ouais, je t'emmènerai
Sur le Scenic Railway
Mais ces émotions-là
C'est facile

Ouais, je t'emmènerai
Sur le Scenic Railway
Et cesse de bouder
C'est d'accord

Je t'y verrai ainsi
Que je te veux, cruelle
Agrippée à mon bras
Par tes ongles blessé

Ouais je vais te sembler
Un peu cynique, ouais ouais
Y'a pas que les machines
Pour s'envoyer en l'air

Paroles et musique
Serge Gainsbourg
© Warner Chappell Music
France/Melody Nelson
Publishing

AMOUR SANS AMOUR — LOVELESS LOVE [1963]

The title Gainsbourg chose for this song is a direct translation of W.C. Handy's[43] *Loveless Love*, which in turn draws inspiration from the jazz and blues standard *Careless Love.** Gainsbourg probably first discovered *Loveless Love* through Billie Holiday's[44] 1940 recording.**

When composing these lyrics, Gainsbourg had just met his second wife, Françoise-Antoinette "Béatrice" Pancrazzi, whom he would divorce in 1966.* Serge and Béatrice had two children: Natacha (born in 1964) and Paul (born in 1968).

I've known countless
Unknowns[45]
All undressed in roses[46]
Countless of these flowers
Barely touched
Blossom diffidently, only to die

Countless tears and necklaces
Strewn at the foot of my bed
What drama
What troubles
For such delicate[47] gemstones

Loveless love
Loveless love
Love without love
And without a face
Loveless love
Love without love
Without illusions, without storms

---

43 William Christopher Handy (1873-1958), known as the "Father of the Blues" for firmly establishing the genre on the national stage, was an American composer and musician.

44 Billie Holiday (1915-1959) was an American jazz singer, songwriter, and actress.

45 Note that Gainsbourg uses the word "inconnues" (feminine and plural form of the noun meaning an unknown, a stranger).

46 In French, "rose" means "pink" when used as an adjective, but means "rose" (the flower) when used as a noun. There is also no difference in pronunciation between "rose" and "roses" in French. As a result, this verse is wonderfully complex: Gainsbourg probably meant for the listener to infer, at first listen, that the "unknowns" were "all undressed in pink", which is a clever play on dress color and skin tone. However, by exploiting the homonymy of the word "rose", this verse ultimately serves as an *après coup* introduction to the rest of the stanza, during which the "unknown" women are compared to the delicate flower.

47 The adjective used by Gainsbourg is "frêle", which translates literally as "frail".

AMOUR SANS AMOUR

Combien j'ai connu
D'inconnues
Toutes de rose dévêtues
Combien de ces fleurs
Qu'on effleure
Et qui s'entrouvrent, puis se meurent

Que de larmes et de colliers
Au pied de mon lit ont roulé
Que de comédies
Que d'ennuis
Pour de si frêles pierreries

Amour sans amour
Amour sans amour
L'amour sans amour
Et sans visage
Amour sans amour
Amour sans amour
Sans illusion, sans orage

Puppy love[48]
How could I
Have forgotten your spells
Love at random
With one look
Erased you from my memory

Of the garden I pillaged
Where the plants have ceased to grow
Nothing remains
I fear
But scentless brambles

Loveless love
Loveless love
Loveless love
Nothing is gloomier
Loveless love
Love without love
But who can exist without love

I've known countless
Unknowns
All undressed in roses

48   Literally translated, this verse would read: "junior-high love".

Amour de collège
Comment ai-je
Pu oublier tes sortilèges
L'amour au hasard
D'un regard
T'a effacé de ma mémoire

Du jardin que j'ai saccagé
Dont les herbes se sont couchées
Il ne reste rien
Je le crains
Que ronces mortes, sans parfum

Amour sans amour
Amour sans amour
Amour sans amour
Rien n'est plus triste
Amour sans amour
Amour sans amour
Mais qui sans amour existe

Combien j'ai connu
D'inconnues
Toutes de roses dévêtues

Paroles et musique Serge Gainsbourg
© 1989 by Melody Nelson Publishing

NO NO THANKS NO [1963]

This is one of Gainsbourg's few politically charged songs. It describes a (seemingly Black) death row inmate's last moments before execution, as he politely refuses a last cigarette, drink, and prayer.

No, no thanks no
I only smoke marijuana
No, no thanks no
It's no use insisting
No, no thanks no
My last cigarette
No, no thanks no
Is already cold

No, no thanks no
I only drink bourbon
No, no thanks no
It's a matter of taste
No, no thanks no
I drank my last glass
No, no thanks no
With Rosemary

No, no thanks no
For me, no prayers
No, no thanks no
God has forsaken me
No, no thanks no
I'll be mourned tomorrow
No, no thanks no
By my Harlem brothers

NO NO THANKS NO

No, no thanks, no
Je n'fume qu'la marijuana
No, no thanks, no
À quoi bon insister
No, no thanks, no
Ma dernière cigarette
No, no thanks, no
Est déjà refroidie

No, no thanks, no
Je n'aime que le bourbon
No, no thanks, no
C'est une affaire de goût
No, no thanks, no
Mon dernier verre je l'ai vidé
No, no thanks, no
Avec Rosemary

No, no thanks, no
Pour moi, pas de prières
No, no thanks, no
Dieu m'a abandonné
No, no thanks, no
Je serai pleuré demain
No, no thanks, no
Par mes frères de Harlem

Paroles et musique Serge Gainsbourg
© 1989 by Melody Nelson Publishing

COULEUR CAFÉ — COFFEE COLOR [1964]

Set to a samba rhythm and riddled with wordplay, this song's lyrics explore the semantic field of coffee while evoking love with a mixed race woman.

HIM – I love your coffee color
Your coffee hair
Your coffee breasts
I love when you dance for me
So that I hear all your
Bracelets jingling
Pretty bracelets
They hula-hoop around your ankles

CHORISTS – Coffee color
How I love your coffee color

HIM – It's crazy how pronounced
The effect is on me
When I see you roll
Your eyes and your hips that way
If like coffee you do nothing
But rile me up
But excite me
Tonight will be sleepless

Chorus

HIM – Not to dwell on it but love
Is like coffee
Its effect wears off quickly
But what would you have me do about it
Everyone's had it with coffee[49]
And it's over
In order to forget it all
We wait for everything to settle down[50]

Chorus x2

---

49 The French lyrics contain an untranslatable play on words. "On en a marre de…" means "we've had it with…" and "marc de café" means "coffee grounds". There is no difference in pronunciation between "marre" and "marc".

50 Another untranslatable play on words. "Attendre que ça se tasse" is a colloquial way of saying "waiting for it to blow over" or "waiting for it to settle down". Note that "tasse" also means "coffee cup".

COULEUR CAFÉ

Lui – J'aime ta couleur café
Tes cheveux café
Ta gorge café
J'aime quand pour moi tu danses
Alors j'entends murmurer
Tous tes bracelets
Jolis bracelets
À tes pieds ils se balancent

**Chœurs – Couleur café
Que j'aime ta couleur café**

Lui – C'est quand même fou l'effet
L'effet que ça fait
De te voir rouler
Ainsi des yeux et des hanches
Si tu fais comme le café
Rien qu'à m'énerver
Rien qu'à m'exciter
Ce soir la nuit sera blanche

Refrain

Lui – L'amour sans philosopher
C'est comme le café
Très vite passé
Mais que veux-tu que j'y fasse
On en a marre de café
Et c'est terminé
Pour tout oublier
On attend que ça se tasse

Refrain bissé

Paroles et musique de Serge Gainsbourg
© Melody Nelson Publishing & Editions et Productions Sidonie

CES PETITS RIENS — THOSE SWEET NOTHINGS [1964]

A bossa nova rhythm is the backdrop to a subtle song about a relationship gone awry and the protagonist's struggle to move on from his flame. *Ces petits riens* is a favorite of female singers and has been covered by, among others, Jane Birkin, Françoise Hardy, Zizi Jeanmaire, and Stacey Kent.*

Better to think of nothing
Than not to think at all
Nothing is already, nothing
Is already quite something
We remember nothing
And since we forget everything
Nothing is much better, nothing
Is much better than everything

Better to think of nothing
Than to think of you
It doesn't buy me anything
It doesn't buy me anything at all
But as though it were
Nothing, I think of all
The sweet nothings
That came to me from you

If there were next to nothing
Next to nothing between us
Evidently
That wouldn't be much
It's those sweet nothings
That I've arranged end to end
Those sweet nothings
That came to me from you

Better to cry over nothing
Than to laugh about everything
Crying over nothing
Is already quite something
But you, you have nothing
In your heart, and it's true
I do envy you
I do resent you

These are the sweet nothings
That came to me from you
Would you like them
Here! What do you expect
Me, I want nothing

CES PETITS RIENS

Mieux vaut n'penser à rien
Que ne pas penser du tout
Rien c'est déjà, rien
C'est déjà beaucoup
On se souvient de rien
Et puisqu'on oublie tout
Rien c'est bien mieux, rien
C'est bien mieux que tout

Mieux vaut n'penser à rien
Que de penser à vous
Ça n'me vaut rien
Ça n'me vaut rien du tout
Mais comme si de rien
N'était, je pense à tous
Ces petits riens
Qui me venaient de vous

Si c'était trois fois rien
Trois fois rien entre nous
Évidemment
Ça ne fait pas beaucoup
Ce sont ces petits riens
Que j'ai mis bout à bout
Ces petits riens
Qui me venaient de vous

Mieux vaut pleurer de rien
Que de rire de tout
Pleurer pour un rien
C'est déjà beaucoup
Mais vous, vous n'avez rien
Dans le cœur, et j'avoue
Je vous envie
Je vous en veux beaucoup

Ce sont ces petits riens
Qui me venaient de vous
Les voulez-vous
Tenez ! Que voulez-vous
Moi, je ne veux pour rien

More to do with you
To be yours
One must be half-mad

Au monde plus rien de vous
Pour être à vous
Faut être à moitié fou

Paroles et musique Serge Gainsbourg
© 1964 Raoul Breton

YÉ-YÉ MANIA

"Yé-yé" was a style of music that emerged in France in the early 1960's. Drawing its name from the "yeah, yeah" interjections commonly found in British and American pop music, it was essentially a copy-cat movement that adapted English-language hits to better suit the French palate.

So popular was the movement that on June 22nd, 1963, over 150,000 youths gathered at the Place de la Nation in Paris for a free concert where numerous pop stars took the stage. 3,000 police officers were called in to keep the peace. A few days later, a sociologist writing for the French daily *Le Monde* dubbed the attendees "yé-yé's", and the name stuck.

Around the same period, Gainsbourg was seen by the general public as a staid singer who had yet to get with the times. He largely eschewed the yé-yé style, although he understood that there was money in it. He began writing bubblegum pop songs (though often rife with innuendo) for stars of the movement such as France Gall and Petula Clark, all the while holding himself to a higher standard when it came to his own albums. When asked why he began writing such songs, Serge would often reply: *"So as not to die of hunger."*[51]

This dichotomy would later be laid bare in *Docteur Jekyll et Monsieur Hyde* [1966], a song which in turn foreshadows the birth of Serge's destructive alter-ego, Gainsbarre.[52]

---

51 Gainsbourg, Verlant, **2000**, Albin Michel.

52 For more on Gainsbarre, see introductory notes to the final chapter: *Enter Gainsbarre: To Synths, Afrobeat, and Funk.*

LES SUCETTES — LOLLIPOPS [1966]

The inspiration for Gainsbourg's "Annie" may have been Annie Chancel, a French yé-yé singer whose stage name is "Sheila" and whose parents sold candy at markets in the suburbs of Paris.** In 1962, at the age of 17, she had a #1 hit in France with the wholesome track *L'école est finie*.

Les sucettes was first sung by France Gall, who was allegedly still innocent enough not to pick up on the lyrics' heavy innuendo. Gall had previously won the Eurovision contest in 1965 with the excellent *Poupée de cire, poupée de son*, another Gainsbourg song that riffed on the naïveté of young female yé-yé singers.

On October 1st, 1966, Gall sang *Les sucettes* on the TV show *Au risque de vous plaire*. Gall cheerfully posed with an oversized, elongated lollipop while four dancers dressed as giant versions of the candy strutted about. To render the production all the more joyfully obscene, viewers were often treated to quick shots of young women sucking on lollipops while gazing longingly into the camera.

A true testament to the song's versatility, *Les sucettes* was one of your translator's favorite lullabies as a child.

> Annie likes lollipops
> Aniseed lollipops
> Annie's
> Aniseed lollipops
> Make her kisses
> Taste like aniseed
> And when the barley sugar
> Infused with aniseed
> Runs down Annie's throat
> She is in heaven

> **For a few pennies**
> **Annie**
> **Buys her aniseed**
> **Lollipops**
> **They are the color of her doe eyes**
> **The color of happy days**

> Annie likes lollipops
> Aniseed lollipops
> Annie's
> Aniseed lollipops
> Make her kisses
> Taste like aniseed
> And when only the little stick
> Remains on her tongue
> She up and runs

LES SUCETTES

Annie aime les sucettes
Les sucettes à l'anis
Les sucettes à l'anis
D'Annie
Donnent à ses baisers
Un goût ani-
Sé lorsque le sucre d'orge
Parfumé à l'anis
Coule dans la gorge d'Annie
Elle est au paradis

Pour quelques pennies
Annie
A ses sucettes à
L'anis
Elles ont la couleur de ses grands yeux
La couleur des jours heureux

Annie aime les sucettes
Les sucettes à l'anis
Les sucettes à l'anis
D'Annie
Donnent à ses baisers
Un goût ani-
Sé lorsqu'elle n'a sur sa langue
Que le petit bâton
Elle prend ses jambes à son corps

Back to the drugstore

Chorus

When the barley sugar
Infused with aniseed
Runs down Annie's throat
She is in heaven

Et retourne au drugstore

Refrain

Lo-orsque le sucre d'orge
Parfumé à l'anis
Coule dans la gorge d'Annie
Elle est au paradis

Paroles et musique Serge Gainsbourg
© Editions & Productions Sidonie

SHU BA DU BA LOO BA [1966]

A song meant to dance the jerk to.* A band based in Los Angeles called The Larks popularized this dance in 1964, when they came out with a track called *The Jerk*. It was similar to the monkey, which was the summer dance craze of 1963 (see Major Lance's excellent song *Monkey Time)*.

Also, in 1966, talking stuffed animals were a novelty.*

HIM – I bought Anna
A fantastic gadget
A stuffed animal
That makes puppy eyes at her

When she pulls…
CHORISTS – SHU BA DU BA LOO BA!
HIM – On the string…
CHORISTS – SHU BA DU BA LOO BA!
HIM – He answers her…
CHORISTS – SHU BA DU BA LOO BA!
HIM – It's driving me crazy

Now Anna and I
Are never alone
He's there on the pillow
Making puppy eyes at her

When she pulls…
CHORISTS – SHU BA DU BA LOO BA!
HIM – On the string…
CHORISTS – SHU BA DU BA LOO BA!
HIM – It goes on and on…
CHORISTS – SHU BA DU BA LOO BA!
HIM – He's driving me crazy

Maybe one day Anna
Will grow tired of him
Then I'll be the only one
Making puppy eyes at her

How do I tell her…
CHORISTS – SHU BA DU BA LOO BA!
HIM – That I love her…
CHORISTS – SHU BA DU BA LOO BA!
HIM – When I hear…
CHORISTS – SHU BA DU BA LOO BA!
HIM – It's driving me crazy

SHU BA DU BA LOO BA

Lui – J'ai acheté pour Anna
Un gadget fantastique
Un animal en peluche
Qui lui fait les yeux doux

Quand elle tire…
Chœurs – Shu ba du ba loo ba !
Lui – La ficelle…
Chœurs – Shu ba du ba loo ba !
Lui – Il lui répond…
Chœurs – Shu ba du ba loo ba !
Lui – Ça me rend fou

Maintenant avec Anna
Nous n'sommes plus jamais seuls
Il est là sur l'oreiller
Qui lui fait les yeux doux

Elle lui tire…
Chœurs – Shu ba du ba loo ba !
Lui – La ficelle…
Chœurs – Shu ba du ba loo ba !
Lui – Ça continue…
Chœurs – Shu ba du ba loo ba !
Lui – Il me rend fou

Peut-être qu'un jour Anna
En aura marre de lui
Alors je serai le seul
À lui faire les yeux doux

Comment lui dire…
Chœurs – Shu ba du ba loo ba !
Lui – Que je l'aime…
Chœurs – Shu ba du ba loo ba !
Lui – Lorsque j'entends…
Chœurs – Shu ba du ba loo ba !
Lui – Ça me rend fou

CHORISTS – SHU BA LOO BA!
SHU BA LOO BA!
SHU BA LOO BA!
SHU BA LOO BA!

AAAAAAH!
AAAAAAH!
AAAAAAH!
SHU BA DU BA LOO BA!

Maybe one day Anna
Will grow tired of him
Then I'll be the only one
Making puppy eyes at her

How do I tell her...
CHORISTS – SHU BA DU BA LOO BA!
HIM – That I love her...
CHORISTS – SHU BA DU BA LOO BA!
HIM – When I hear...
CHORISTS – SHU BA DU BA LOO BA!
HIM – It's driving me crazy

CHŒURS – SHU BA LOO BA !
SHU BA LOO BA !
SHU BA LOO BA !
SHU BA LOO BA !

AAAAAAH !
AAAAAAH !
AAAAAAH !
SHU BA DU BA LOO BA !

LUI – Peut-être qu'un jour Anna
En aura marre de lui
Alors je serai le seul
À lui faire les yeux doux

Comment lui dire...
CHŒURS – SHU BA DU BA LOO BA !
LUI – Que je l'aime...
CHŒURS – SHU BA DU BA LOO BA !
LUI – Lorsque j'entends...
CHŒURS – SHU BA DU BA LOO BA !
LUI – Ça me rend fou

Paroles et musique Serge Gainsbourg

MARILU [1966]

This song may be an homage to the Italian actress Marilù Tolo, although this has never been confirmed. Another rumor is that Tolo's agent refused to allow Gainsbourg to title the work *Marilu Tolo*.*

In this translator's opinion, *Marilu* is one of Gainsbourg's most underrated songs. Initially disquieting undertones give way to a (possibly) sweet outcome.

CHORISTS – Marilu
Marilu

HIM – Tell me Marilu
Would you Marilu
Answer this question?
If you don't want to just say no
I won't hold a grudge

I know Marilu
That with Marilu
One can't go too far
Or else she gets upset
And I don't want that

Have you ever loved Marilu?
Might you have tried Marilu?
Would I be the first Marilu?
Answer me Marilu

Tell me Marilu
I will Marilu
Repeat my question for you
You aren't paying attention
I'm not surprised

I know Marilu
That with Marilu
One must be patient
She's a little girl
Who doesn't listen to me

Chorus

Tell me Marilu
Why Marilu
You train your eyes on the floor like that
When you have such pretty ones
Come now, look at me

MARILU

CHŒURS – Marilu
Marilu

LUI – Dis-moi Marilu
Veux-tu Marilu
Répondre à cette question
Si tu n'veux pas tu dis non
Je ne t'en voudrai pas

Je sais Marilu
Qu'avec Marilu
Il n'faut pas trop insister
Sinon elle va se fâcher
Et ça je ne veux pas

As-tu déjà aimé Marilu
Aurais-tu essayé Marilu
Serais-je le premier Marilu
Réponds-moi Marilu

Dis-moi Marilu
Je vais Marilu
Te répéter ma question
Tu ne fais pas attention
Ça ne m'étonne pas

Je sais Marilu
Qu'avec Marilu
Il faut se montrer patient
C'est une petite enfant
Qui ne m'écoute pas

Refrain

Dis-moi Marilu
Pourquoi Marilu
Baisses-tu les yeux ainsi
Toi qui les as si jolis
Allons regarde-moi

I know Marilu
That with Marilu
Other boys have danced
But whatever are you crying for
So that's what it was

You have already loved, Marilu
You have indeed tried, Marilu
I'll be the last one, Marilu
No worries, Marilu

No, no worries Marilu
No, don't cry Marilu
No, don't cry, Marilu

Je sais Marilu
Qu'avec Marilu
D'autres garçons ont dansé
Mais qu'as-tu donc à pleurer
Ainsi c'était donc ça

Tu as déjà aimé Marilu
Tu as donc essayé Marilu
Je serai le dernier Marilu
Ça n'fait rien Marilu

Non, ça n'fait rien Marilu
Non, ne pleure pas Marilu
Non, ne pleure pas Marilu

Paroles et musique Serge Gainsbourg
© Warner Chappell Music France/Melody Nelson Publishing

BABY POP [1966]

Yet another song written for France Gall (see also *Les sucettes*). This one boasts dark lyrics juxtaposed with an uplifting melody. Gainsbourg warns the blithe younger generation of hard times ahead in the Cold War era.

The few pennies you'll earn
You'll have to work hard for, ye-ye-ye
Wake up at dawn
Fall through summer

You can save all you want
It'll never amount to anything, ye-ye-ye
And with those meager funds
You'll be lucky to even go dancing

Sing, dance, Baby Pop
As though tomorrow, Baby Pop
Were to never, Baby Pop
Never come again

Sing, dance, Baby Pop
As though tomorrow, Baby Pop
At first light, Baby Pop
You were going to die

You concoct theories on love
Someday it will happen, ye-ye-ye
You'll be a poor kid
Alone and abandoned

You'll end up marrying
Perhaps even against your will, ye-ye-ye
And on your wedding night
It'll be too late for second thoughts

Chorus

You can't be blind to the danger
Posed by freedom, ye-ye-ye
The threat of war
Looms large on the horizon

At this very moment Baby you know
Where all the suns will rise, ye-ye-ye
Somewhere on Earth
Bullets fly blood is spilled

BABY POP

Les quelques sous que tu vas gagner
Faudra pour ça durement travailler, yéi-yéi-yé
Te lever aux aurores
Automne comme été

Tu auras beau économiser
Tu n'pourras rien mettre de côté, yéi-yéi-yé
Et là-dessus encore
Heureuse si tu peux aller danser

Chante, danse, Baby Pop
Comme si demain, Baby Pop
Ne devait jamais, Baby Pop
Jamais revenir

Chante, danse, Baby Pop
Comme si demain, Baby Pop
Au petit matin, Baby Pop
Tu devais mourir

Sur l'amour tu te fais des idées
Un jour ou l'autre c'est obligé, yéi-yéi-yé
Tu seras une pauvre gosse
Seule et abandonnée

Tu finiras par te marier
Peut-être même contre ton gré, yéi-yéi-yé
À la nuit de tes noces
Il sera trop tard pour le regretter

Refrain

Tu ne peux ignorer les dangers
Que représentent les libertés, yéi-yéi-yé
Les menaces de guerre
Semblent se préciser

À cet instant Baby tu le sais
Où tous les soleils vont se lever, yéi-yéi-yé
Quelque part sur la terre
Les balles sifflent le sang est versé

Chorus

Refrain

Paroles et musique Serge Gainsbourg
© Sidonie

DOCTEUR JEKYLL ET MONSIEUR HYDE – DR. JEKYLL AND MR. HYDE [1966]

This landmark song foreshadows the gradual metamorphosis from Gainsbourg to Gainsbarre[53], the controversial alcoholic that Serge would become right around the time of his breakup with Jane Birkin.

CHORISTS – Hello Dr. Jekyll
HIM – No, I'm not Dr. Jekyll
CHORISTS – Hello Dr. Jekyll
HIM – My name is Hyde, Mr. Hyde[54]

Dr. Jekyll was possessed
By Mr. Hyde, who was his evil twin
Mr. Hyde never said anything
But secretly thought little of him

CHORISTS – Hello Dr. Jekyll
HIM – I'm telling you I'm not Dr. Jekyll
CHORISTS – Hello Dr. Jekyll
HIM – My name is Hyde, Mr. Hyde

Dr. Jekyll was only ever with
Bitches who couldn't care less about him
In his heart Mr. Hyde
Took notes for the doctor

CHORISTS – Hello Dr. Jekyll
HIM – Dr. Jekyll is no more
CHORISTS – Hello Dr. Jekyll
HIM – My name is Hyde, Mr. Hyde

One day Dr. Jekyll came to the realization
That Mr. Hyde was what people liked about him
Mr. Hyde, that bastard
Did away with

HIM & CHORISTS – Dr. Jekyll
CHORISTS – Dr. Jekyll
HIM – ...
CHORISTS – Dr. Jekyll
HIM – ...
CHORISTS – Dr. Jekyll
HIM – ...

---

53 For more on Gainsbarre, see introductory notes to the last chapter: *Enter Gainsbarre: To Synths, Afrobeat, and Funk.*

54 The first James Bond movie, *Dr. No*, was released in 1962. This verse may well have been inspired by the famous line: "My name is Bond. James Bond."

DOCTEUR JEKYLL ET MONSIEUR HYDE

CHŒURS – Hello Docteur Jekyll
LUI – Non, je n'suis pas le Docteur Jekyll
CHŒURS – Hello Docteur Jekyll
LUI – Mon nom est Hyde, Mister Hyde

Docteur Jekyll il avait en lui
Un Monsieur Hyde qui était son mauvais génie
Mister Hyde ne disait rien
Mais en secret n'en pensait pas moins

CHŒURS – Hello Docteur Jekyll
LUI – Je vous dis que je n'suis pas le Docteur Jekyll
CHŒURS – Hello Docteur Jekyll
LUI – Que mon nom est Hyde, Mister Hyde

Docteur Jekyll n'a eu dans sa vie
Que de petites garces qui se foutaient de lui
Mister Hyde dans son cœur
Prenait des notes pour le docteur

CHŒURS – Hello Docteur Jekyll
LUI – Il n'y'a plus de Docteur Jekyll
CHŒURS – Hello Docteur Jekyll
LUI – Mon nom est Hyde, Mister Hyde

Docteur Jekyll un jour a compris
Que c'est ce Monsieur Hyde qu'on aimait en lui
Mister Hyde, ce salaud
A fait la peau, la peau du

LUI & CHŒURS – Docteur Jekyll
CHŒURS – Docteur Jekyll
LUI – ...
CHŒURS – Docteur Jekyll
LUI – ...
CHŒURS – Docteur Jekyll
LUI – ...

CHORISTS – Dr. Jekyll
HIM – ...

CHŒURS – Docteur Jekyll
LUI – ...

Paroles et musique Serge Gainsbourg
© Editions & Productions Sidonie

BETWEEN LIFE AND LOVE: ANNA, THE MUSICAL

Pierre Koralnik's *Anna* was first broadcast on January 13th, 1967, at the dawn of the color-TV era. The soundtrack to the musical was written entirely by Gainsbourg. With fifteen days remaining before the start of filming, Serge had only completed half the required tracks. Eight straight nights of self-imposed insomnia – his personal record – were required to get back on schedule. For Serge could not focus solely on writing: he had committed to a part in the French TV show *Vidocq,* and was also heavily involved in singing lessons given to *Anna's* stars, Jean-Claude Brialy and Anna Karina. Karina was twenty-seven years old at the time but had already achieved icon status through her work with Jean-Luc Godard, the radical *nouvelle vague* director whom she had divorced only a couple years prior.[55]

The soundtrack to *Anna* is quite avant-garde in that it marks the emergence of French rock as an independent form. At a time when the ersatz yé-yé style was the best the country had to offer its citizens, *Anna* laid bare Gainsbourg's contempt for the movement. Tracks like *Boomerang, Un poison violent c'est ça l'amour (A Terrible Poison That's What Love Is)* and *Roller Girl* are some of the earliest examples of French rock. Serge said it best, if somewhat boastfully: *"It was French rock before French rock existed, really."*[56] Shrewd listeners will note that *Roller Girl* evokes two themes – comic strips and Harley Davidson motorcycles – that Serge would further flesh out with Brigitte Bardot during their brief romance.

Deprived of four tracks from the film due to size constraints, the soundtrack was released in January of 1967.

55 Gainsbourg, Verlant, **2000**, Albin Michel.
56 Gainsbourg, Verlant, **2000**, Albin Michel.

SOUS LE SOLEIL EXACTEMENT — UNDER THE SUN EXACTLY [1967]

This beautiful number has become the most popular song off the *Anna* soundtrack. Anna Karina's innocently erotic singing style prefigures Jane Birkin's work with Serge, who re-recorded the song on the 1969 album *Jane Birkin et Serge Gainsbourg.*

A precise location under the Tropic
Of Capricorn, or Cancer[57]
I've since forgotten which one

Under the sun, exactly
Not beside it, not any which spot
Under the sun, under the sun exactly
Right below it

In what country, in what district?
It was right by the ocean
I've since forgotten which one

Chorus

Was it New Mexico
Toward Cape Horn, toward Cap-Vert
Was it on an archipelago?

Chorus

Surely it's an erotic dream
That I'm having eyes wide open
And yet what if it were real

Chorus[58]

Tomorrow, I'll return to the same spot
Under the sun
And the tide will claim me
Until its next voyage back to shore
It will be lovely
But it's due to these daydreams
That I find myself here
Period, full stop
And one can get used to anything
Isn't that right, Anna

---

57   These may be references to Henry Miller's *Tropic of Cancer* (1934) and *Tropic of Capricorn* (1939).** Both were written in Paris. Deemed obscene, the novels were banned in the United States until the early 1960's.

58   The following lines (in italics) are only spoken in *Anna,* Koralnik's film. They are not present in the soundtrack version of the song.

SOUS LE SOLEIL EXACTEMENT

Un point précis sous le tropique
Du Capricorne, ou du Cancer
Depuis, j'ai oublié lequel

Sous le soleil exactement
Pas à côté, pas n'importe où
Sous le soleil, sous le soleil exactement
Juste en dessous

Dans quel pays, dans quel district?
C'était tout au bord de la mer
Depuis, j'ai oublié laquelle

Refrain

Était-ce le Nouveau-Mexique
Vers le cap Horn, vers le cap Vert
Était-ce sur un archipel?

Refrain

C'est sûrement un rêve érotique
Que je me fais les yeux ouverts
Et pourtant si c'était réel

Refrain

Demain je reviendrai au même endroit
Sous le soleil
Et la mer m'emportera
Jusqu'à son prochain retour
Ce sera formidable
Mais avec des si
Je suis ici
Un point c'est tout
Et l'on s'accommode de tout
N'est-ce pas, Anna

Paroles et musique Serge Gainsbourg
© Warner Chappell Music France/Melody Nelson Publishing

NE DIS RIEN — SAY NOTHING [1967]

A slow waltz frames this magnificent piece in which Anna Karina finishes the short verses begun by Jean-Claude Brialy and Gainsbourg.

The shadowy *Anna* scene set to this track features Karina and Brialy passing each other by on moving pedestrian walkways in a dimly lit Paris metro station. It would not have looked the least bit out of place in Hungarian director Nimród Antal's 2003 underworld cult classic, *Kontroll,* which was shot entirely in the Budapest metro.

BRIALY – *You're nuts! Nuts!*
Staying put is the only way to move around here
Or maybe I ought to break my neck and kill myself!
Seriously, do you see what you've done to me?
Do you see what's left of me?
Nothing! Lord Nothing!

Jesus, what the hell is she doing?
Is she here, is she not here?
This can't be!
It can't! It can't!
And yet
I need only close my eyes for you to appear

THEM – Say
HER – Nothing
THEM – Whatever
HER – You do
THEM – Say
HER – Nothing
THEM – Follow me

THEM – Say
HER – Nothing
THEM – Be not
HER – Afraid
THEM – I am
HER – Not to
THEM – Fear

ALL – Follow me 'til the end of the night
'Til the end of my madness
Leave time behind, forget tomorrow
Forget everything, leave your thoughts behind

THEM – Say
HER – Nothing
THEM – Whatever

NE DIS RIEN

BRIALY – *Ça va pas ! Ça va pas !*
Rester immobile, seule façon ici de se mouvoir
Ou alors je m'casse la gueule, et je m'tue !
Non mais, t'as vu c'que t'as fait d'moi ?
T'as vu c'qu'il en reste ?
Nothing ! Lord Nothing !

Mais qu'est-ce qu'elle fait bon Dieu ?
Elle est là, elle est pas là ?
C'est pas possible !
Pas possible ! Pas possible !
Et pourtant
Il m'suffit d' fermer les yeux et tu es là

Eux – Ne dis
Elle – Rien
Eux – Surtout
Elle – Pas
Eux – Ne dis
Elle – Rien
Eux – Suis-moi

Eux – Ne dis
Elle – Rien
Eux – N'aie pas
Elle – Peur
Eux – Ne crains
Elle – Rien
Eux – De moi

Tous – Suis-moi jusqu'au bout de la nuit
Jusqu'au bout de ma folie
Laisse le temps, oublie demain
Oublie tout, ne pense plus à rien

Eux – Ne dis
Elle – Rien
Eux – Surtout

HER – You do
THEM – Say
HER – Nothing
THEM – Follow me

THEM – Say
HER – Nothing
THEM – Be not
HER – Afraid
THEM – I am
HER – Not to
THEM – Fear

Chorus

HER – La la la
La la la
La la la la la
La la la
La la la
La la la la la

Chorus

Elle – Pas
Eux – Ne dis
Elle – Rien
Eux – Suis-moi

Eux – Ne dis
Elle – Rien
Eux – N'aie pas
Elle – Peur
Eux – Ne crains
Elle – Rien
Eux – De moi

Refrain

Elle – La la la
La la la
La la la la la
La la la
La la la
La la la la la

Refrain

Paroles et musique Serge Gainsbourg
© Warner Chappell Music France/Melody Nelson Publishing

THE BARDOT EFFECT

It all began in October of 1967. Brigitte Bardot was thirty-three, married to German millionaire Gunther Sachs, and at her most beautiful. For months she had been preparing for her smash-hit TV special *Le Show Bardot,* which was to be broadcast on January 1st, 1968.

Serge invites himself over to Brigitte's apartment to play *Harley Davidson* on the piano, with the hope that she will deem it worthy of inclusion in her TV special. Brigitte is initially quite reticent, as she doesn't particularly care for motorcycles. The moment must have been made all the more awkward by Brigitte's stage fright: *"I didn't dare sing in front of him. There was something in the way he looked at me that made me freeze up. A sort of timid insolence, like he was waiting, with a hint of superior humility. He was full of strange contradictions, a scornful glare in an otherwise sad face, a cold humor betrayed by a warmth in his eyes."*[59] Thankfully, a bottle of Moët & Chandon saved the day, and Serge would end up placing a half-dozen songs on the 50-minute special.

Later in October, at a dinner with friends, Brigitte grasps Serge's hand under the table. The two lock eyes and their dinner companions promptly excuse themselves.

One night, Brigitte asks Serge to write her the most beautiful love song he can imagine. So he writes two: *Bonnie and Clyde and Je t'aime moi non plus.* In her autobiography, Bardot reflects on the recording session for the latter: *"When we recorded* Je t'aime moi non plus *it was late at night, at the Barclay studios. We each had a mic. We were maybe three feet away from each other, holding hands. I was a little ashamed about imitating the lovemaking between Serge and me, sighing in desire like I was coming, all in front of the engineers. But after all, I was simply interpreting a situation, as if it were a film I was shooting. Then Serge comforted me with a wink, a smile, and a kiss. It was great, beautiful, pure. It was us."*[60]

Thus far, Gunther Sachs had paid the affair no mind. But he couldn't ignore this recording. On the morning of December 12th, Brigitte panicked and sent Serge a letter that he would later display among other souvenirs at his home on the rue de Verneuil. "It is perched atop a lectern: on letterhead that reads 'Brigitte Sachs Bardot', the following

---

59 Initiales B.B., Bardot, **1996**, Editions Grasset. Translation by Paul Knobloch in Gainsbourg, Verlant, **2000**, Albin Michel.

60 Initiales B.B., Bardot, **1996**, Editions Grasset. Translation by Paul Knobloch in Gainsbourg, Verlant, **2000**, Albin Michel.

can be made out: 'Serge, I implore you to halt the release of *Je t'aime'....*" Sachs had put his foot down. And so it was over, less than two months after it had begun. After gracefully acquiescing to Brigitte's desperate request, Serge spent Christmas alone. [61]

On January 2nd, Brigitte took off for the South of Spain to film *Shalako,* but not before seeing Serge one last time. A final passage from Bardot's autobiography: *"I saw Serge again [at my apartment] while I was packing. Madame Renée, my housekeeper, in strictest confidence, had orders not to open the door for anyone. Serge filled my suitcase with little words of love scribbled over sheets of music [...]. At the last moment, I pierced the skin of my right index finger and wrote 'Je t'aime' in blood. He did the same and wrote 'moi non plus.' Then we melted into each other's tears, hands, mouths, breath.'*[62]

*Serge and Brigitte Bardot in the studio preparing for the latter's
1968 TV special* Le Show Bardot.

Photo by Patrice Habans

---

61 Gainsbourg, Verlant, **2000**, Albin Michel.
62 Gainsbourg, Verlant, **2000**, Albin Michel. Translation adapted from that of Paul Knobloch.

HARLEY DAVIDSON [1967]

This song marks the very beginning of Gainsbourg's torrid affair with Brigitte Bardot. The accompanying *Le Show Bardot* clip features Bardot mounting a classic Harley in a leather miniskirt and thigh-high boots.

Another reference to the famed American motorcycle manufacturer would come later, in the 1984 track *Harley Davidson of a Bitch*.

I don't need anyone
When I'm riding my Harley Davidson
I don't recognize anyone
When I'm riding my Harley Davidson

When I fire up the hog
I'm no longer of this Earth
If I go to heaven
It'll be at one hell of a pace

Chorus

And if I die tomorrow
Such was my destiny
I cherish life much less
Than I do my fearsome bike

Chorus

On the road when I feel
The motor's vibrations
Desire begins to mount
Deep within my loins

Chorus

I'm going over a hundred
I might crash and burn
I couldn't care less about dying
When my hair's blowing in the wind
I couldn't care less about dying
When my hair's blowing in the wind

HARLEY DAVIDSON

Je n'ai besoin de personne
En Harley Davidson
Je n'reconnais plus personne
En Harley Davidson

J'appuie sur le starter
Et voici que je quitte la terre
J'irai peut-être au paradis
Mais dans un train d'enfer

Refrain

Et si je meurs demain
C'est que tel était mon destin
Je tiens bien moins à la vie
Qu'à mon terrible engin

Refrain

Quand je sens en chemin
Les trépidations de ma machine
Il me monte des désirs
Dans le creux de mes reins

Refrain

Je vais à plus de cent
Et je me sens à feu et à sang
Que m'importe de mourir
Les cheveux dans le vent
Que m'importe de mourir
Les cheveux dans le vent

Paroles et musique Serge Gainsbourg

BONNIE AND CLYDE [1967]

Bonnie Parker and Clyde Barrow, two of America's most infamous gangsters, died in a hail of police bullets on May 23rd, 1934.

At the time of this song's writing, Arthur Penn's film celebrating their life had just come out in the United States, and the French release was set for January 1968.*

Brigitte plays the role of Bonnie Parker in this timeless duet, which she and Serge sang on *Le Show Bardot*.

Note that an English version of this song exists: set to the same music as the original, it is sung only by Gainsbourg, and the lyrics are excerpts taken from Bonnie Parker's poem *The Trail's End* (1934).

HIM – *You've read the story of Jesse James*
How he lived, how he died
You liked it, huh, you want more
Well! Then, listen to the story of Bonnie and Clyde

Now then, Clyde has a girlfriend
She is beautiful, and her name is... HER – *Bonnie*
HIM – Together they make up the Barrow gang
Their names... HER – Bonnie Parker... HIM – and Clyde Barrow

TOGETHER – Bonnie and Clyde
Bonnie and Clyde

HER – *Me, back when I knew Clyde*
He was a loyal, honest, and upstanding guy
HIM – One has to think society
Is what corrupted me

TOGETHER – Bonnie and Clyde
Bonnie and Clyde

HIM – *You name it, they've written it about us*
HER – *People say we kill in cold blood*
HIM – It's no fun, yet we have no choice but
HER – To shut the squealers up

TOGETHER – Bonnie and Clyde
Bonnie and Clyde

HIM – *Every time a cop gets whacked*
HER – *Or a business or bank gets held up*
HIM – For the police, it's obviously
HER – The work of... HIM – Clyde Barrow... HER – Bonnie Parker

BONNIE AND CLYDE

Lui – *Vous avez lu l'histoire de Jesse James*
Comment il vécut, comment il est mort
Ça vous a plu, hein, vous en demandez encore
Eh ! bien, écoutez l'histoire de Bonnie and Clyde

Alors voilà, Clyde a une petite amie
Elle est belle, et son prénom c'est... Elle – *Bonnie*
Lui – À eux deux ils forment le gang Barrow
Leurs noms... Elle – Bonnie Parker... Lui – et Clyde Barrow

Lui & Elle – Bonnie and Clyde
Bonnie and Clyde

Elle – *Moi, lorsque j'ai connu Clyde autrefois*
C'était un gars loyal, honnête et droit
Lui – Il faut croire que c'est la société
Qui m'a définitivement abîmé

Lui & Elle – Bonnie and Clyde
Bonnie and Clyde

Lui – *Qu'est-ce qu'on n'a pas écrit sur elle et moi*
Elle – *On prétend que nous tuons de sang-froid*
Lui – C'est pas drôle, mais on est bien obligé
Elle – De faire taire celui qui s'met à gueuler

Lui & Elle – Bonnie and Clyde
Bonnie and Clyde

Lui – *Chaque fois qu'un policeman se fait buter*
Elle – *Qu'un garage ou qu'une banque se fait braquer*
Lui – Pour la police, ça ne fait pas d'mystère
Elle – C'est signé... Lui – Clyde Barrow... Elle – Bonnie Parker

TOGETHER – Bonnie and Clyde
Bonnie and Clyde

HIM – *These days, anytime we try to live straight*
HER – *Anytime we try to settle down*
HIM – Not three days go by, before the rat-tat-tat
HER – Of machine gun fire charges back into our lives

TOGETHER – Bonnie and Clyde
Bonnie and Clyde

HIM – *One of these days, we'll fall together*
Personally I don't give a damn, I live for Bonnie
HER – Who cares if they off me
Me Bonnie, I swoon only over Clyde Barrow

TOGETHER – Bonnie and Clyde
Bonnie and Clyde

HIM – *Regardless, they were done for*
HER – *The only way out was to die*
HIM – But countless men followed them to hell
TOGETHER – When Barrow and Bonnie Parker died

Bonnie and Clyde
Bonnie and Clyde

Lui & Elle – Bonnie and Clyde
Bonnie and Clyde

Lui – *Maintenant, chaque fois qu'on essaie d'se ranger*
Elle – *De s'installer tranquilles dans un meublé*
Lui – Dans les trois jours, voilà le tac-tac-tac
Elle – Des mitraillettes qui reviennent à l'attaque

Lui & Elle – Bonnie and Clyde
Bonnie and Clyde

Lui – *Un de ces quatre, nous tomberons ensemble*
Moi je m'en fous, c'est pour Bonnie que je tremble
Elle – Quelle importance qu'ils me fassent la peau
Moi Bonnie, je tremble pour Clyde Barrow

Lui & Elle – Bonnie and Clyde
Bonnie and Clyde

Lui – *De toute façon ils n'pouvaient plus s'en sortir*
Elle – *La seule solution c'était mourir*
Lui – Mais plus d'un les a suivis en enfer
Lui & Elle – Quand sont morts Barrow et Bonnie Parker

Bonnie and Clyde
Bonnie and Clyde

Paroles et musique Serge Gainsbourg
©1967 by Editions et Productions Sidonie/Melody Nelson Publishing

REQUIEM POUR UN CON — REQUIEM FOR AN ASSHOLE [1968]

This song was part of the soundtrack for George Lautner's 1968 film *Le Pacha (The Pasha)**, which was filmed in late 1967 during Serge's romance with Brigitte Bardot.[63]

A dance version of the requiem was commissioned by Gainsbourg's artistic director on December 27th, 1990. Ironically, the singer would pass away on March 2nd, 1991, one day after the remix was completed.*

This is Gainsbourg's second requiem, after 1962's *Requiem pour un twisteur*.

CHORISTS – *One, two, one, two, three*

HIM – Listen to the organ, it's playing for you
Yeah, that melody is ruthless
I hope you like it
It's pretty nice, isn't it
It's the requiem
For an asshole

Yeah, I composed it exclusively for you
To immortalize your heinous ways
It's a lovely tune
Don't you think
It's true to you
You fucking asshole

There goes that organ again
You must learn this score by heart
You must not have
Even the slightest hesitation
When it comes to the requiem
For an asshole

Now you're looking at me, you don't appreciate it
But what part don't you like
Me I couldn't care less
Whether or not you enjoy it
I'm playing it again for you
You fucking asshole

Chorus

Yeah, I composed it exclusively for you
To immortalize your heinous ways
On your blood-drained face

---

63 Gainsbourg, Verlant, **2000**, Albin Michel.

REQUIEM POUR UN CON

CHŒURS – *Un, deux, un, deux, trois*

LUI – Écoute les orgues, elles jouent pour toi
Hein, il est terrible, cet air-là
J'espère que tu aimes
C'est assez beau, non
C'est le requiem
Pour un con

Ouais, je l'ai composé spécialement pour toi
À ta mémoire de scélérat
C'est un joli thème
Tu ne trouves pas, non
Semblable à toi-même
Pauvre con

Voici les orgues qui remettent ça
Faut qu't'apprennes par cœur cet air-là
Que tu n'aies pas même
Une hésitation
Sur le requiem
Pour un con

Quoi tu me regardes, tu n'apprécies pas
Mais qu'est-ce qu'y'a là-dedans qui t'plaît pas
Pour moi c'est idem
Que ça t'plaise ou non
J'te l'rejoue quand même
Pauvre con

Refrain

Ouais, je l'ai composé spécialement pour toi
À ta mémoire de scélérat
Sur ta figure blême

On the prison walls
I myself will carve the words:
"You fucking asshole"

Aux murs des prisons
J'inscrirai moi-même
"Pauvre con"

Paroles Serge Gainsbourg
Musique Serge Gainsbourg et Michel Colombier
© Hortensia

INITIALS BB [1968]

"BB" is a barely-veiled reference to Brigitte Bardot.

Gainsbourg was influenced by Edgar Allen Poe's *The Raven* when writing these lyrics; the opening lines of his song recall those of Poe's famous poem: *Once upon a midnight dreary, while I pondered, weak and weary, / Over many a quaint and curious volume of forgotten lore.* Parallels can also be drawn between Gainsbourg's Bardot and Poe's Lenore, the quintessential lost female love.**

Of Bardot, Gainsbourg said after their break-up: *"Cette fille m'a marqué au fer rouge."* *("That girl branded me like a red-hot iron.")*

The song's melody borrows from a theme found in Antonín Dvořák's *New World* symphony.*

HIM – *One night as I was*
Despondently leafing through
L'Amour Monstre
By Pauwels[64]
In some pub
In the heart of London
A vision appeared to me
In my seltzer water

CHORISTS – B initials
B initials
B initials
BB

HIM – *While the Imperator's*[65] *medals*
Bring out the gleam
Of the bronze and gold
Around her waist
Cold rings of platinum
Etch the stigma of slavery
Onto each
Of her fingers

---

64 Louis Pauwels (1920-1997) was a French author and journalist. *L'Amour Monstre* was on Bardot's nightstand during her relationship with Gainsbourg; she gave him a copy of the novel as a present.**

65 "Imperator" was a title given to Roman emperors. Gainsbourg uses "impérator" rather than the French "empereur", which would have been translated as "emperor".

INITIALS BB

Lui – *Une nuit que j'étais*
À me morfondre
Dans quelque pub anglais
Du cœur de Londres
Parcourant "L'amour mon-
Stre" de Pauwels
Me vint une vision
Dans l'eau de Seltz

Chœurs – B initials
B initials
B initials
BB

Lui – *Tandis que des médailles*
D'impérator
Font briller à sa taille
Le bronze et l'or
Le platine lui grave
D'un cercle froid
La marque des esclaves
À chaque doigt

Chorus

HIM – *Her thigh-high boots*
Form a chalice
Brimming with beauty
She wears
Nothing else
Save for a touch
Of essence de Guerlain
In her hair

Chorus

HIM – *The silver bells*
On her wrists
Echoed every move
She made
Charms jingling
She stepped forward
And uttered a single word
"Almería"[66]

Chorus x2

---

66   The city of Almería was where Shalako, one of Bardot's last movies, was filmed.* The city was synonymous with heartbreak for Gainsbourg, as the couple's torrid romance was never rekindled after Bardot headed to the Southern coast of Spain.

Refrain

LUI – *Jusques en haut des cuisses*
Elle est bottée
Et c'est comme un calice
À sa beauté
Elle ne porte rien
D'autre qu'un peu
D'essence de Guerlain
Dans les cheveux

Refrain

LUI – *À chaque mouvement*
On entendait
Les clochettes d'argent
De ses poignets
Agitant ces grelots
Elle avança
Et prononça ce mot
"Almería"

Refrain bissé

Paroles et musique Serge Gainsbourg
© 1968 Editions & Productions Sidonie & Melody Nelson Publishing

MANON [1968]

Manon finds Gainsbourg sad and spiteful after his breakup with Bardot. "I have to love you together with another", a line from the chorus, seems an unmistakable reference to Bardot's then-husband, Gunther Sachs.

> Manon
> Manon
> No, surely you know not, Manon
> How much I loathe
> What you are
> If you knew
> Manon
> I would have already lost you, Manon
>
> **Depraved Manon**
> **Perfidious Manon**
> **I have to love you together with another**
> **I know it, Manon**
> **Cruel Manon**
>
> Manon
> Manon
> No, you'll never know, Manon
> How much I loathe
> What you are
> In essence
> Manon
> I think I've gone mad
>
> *I love you, Manon*

MANON

Manon
Manon
Non, tu ne sais sûrement pas, Manon
À quel point je hais
Ce que tu es
Sinon
Manon
Je t'aurais déjà perdue, Manon

Perverse Manon
Perfide Manon
Il me faut t'aimer avec un autre
Je le sais, Manon
Cruelle Manon

Manon
Manon
Non, tu ne sauras jamais, Manon
À quel point je hais
Ce que tu es
Au fond
Manon
Je pense avoir perdu la raison

Je t'aime, Manon

Paroles et musique Serge Gainsbourg
© Éden Roc

BLOODY JACK [1967]

Gainsbourg draws inspiration from the mysterious Jack the Ripper murders of 1888, when at least five prostitutes were brutally disemboweled in London. Mary Jane Kelly was widely believed to be the fifth and final victim; her heart was missing from the gory crime scene.

HIM – Bloody Jack's heart
Skips three beats out of four
But under the spell of his soft kisses
Yours beats like mad

HER – Bloody Jack's heart
Skips three beats out of four
But under the spell of his soft kisses
Mine beats like mad

HIM – In the dark, I listen to them beat
I compare our two beats
And to your four beats
Bloody Jack has only one

Chorus

HIM – When pressed against another, a heart beats faster
As though in the grip of fear
But while yours stirs inside you
I can barely hear my heart

Chorus

HIM – Next to mine, your heart seems
More anxious and more passionate
Will I hear them beat together someday
Does Bloody Jack truly have a heart

Chorus

BLOODY JACK

Lui – Le cœur de Bloody Jack
Ne bat qu'un coup sur quatre
Mais sous ses baisers doux
Le tien bat comme un fou

Elle – Le cœur de Bloody Jack
Ne bat qu'un coup sur quatre
Mais sous ses baisers doux
Le mien bat comme un fou

Lui – Dans le noir, je les écoute battre
Je compare nos deux battements
Et tandis que ton cœur en a quatre
Bloody Jack en a un seulement

Refrain

Lui – Cœur contre cœur, le cœur bat plus vite
Comme sous l'emprise de la peur
Mais tandis qu'en toi le tien s'agite
C'est à peine si j'entends mon cœur

Refrain

Lui – À côté du mien, ton cœur me semble
Avoir plus d'angoisse et de ferveur
Les entendrai-je un jour battre ensemble
Bloody Jack a-t-il vraiment un cœur

Refrain

Paroles et musique Serge Gainsbourg
© Warner Chappell Music France/Melody Nelson Publishing

TORREY CANYON [1967]

The *Torrey Canyon* was an oil tanker capable of carrying 120,000 metric tons (roughly 750,000 barrels) of crude oil. It was shipwrecked off the western coast of Cornwall, England on March 18th, 1967, causing an environmental disaster. At the time the *Torrey Canyon* was the largest vessel ever to be wrecked.

The details Gainsbourg provides are all factual. The ship was owned by the Barracuda Tanker Corporation, a subsidiary of the Union Oil Corporation (since acquired by Chevron). It was registered in Liberia, chartered to British Petroleum, and manned by an Italian crew.

> HIM – I was born
> In the Japanese shipyards
> In truth I belong
> To the Americans
> A subsidiary
> Of a shipbuilder
> Whose address I forget
> Based in Los Angeles
>
> **One hundred twenty thousand tons of crude oil**
> **One hundred twenty thousand tons**
> **CHORISTS – In the Torrey Canyon**
> **The Torrey Canyon**
>
> HIM – The islands of Bermuda
> At thirty degrees latitude
> Are home to the Barracuda Tan-
> Ker Corporation
> Its boss
> Leased me to
> The Union Oil Company
> Of California
>
> **One hundred twenty thousand tons of crude oil**
> **One hundred twenty thousand tons**
> **CHORISTS – In the Torrey Canyon**
> **The Torrey Canyon**
>
> HIM – I may fly
> Liberia's flag
> But the captain and crew
> Are all Italian
> The oil
> In my tanks
> Belongs to
> British Petroleum

TORREY CANYON

Lui – Je suis né
Dans les chantiers japonais
En vérité j'appartiens
Aux Américains
Une filiale
D'une compagnie navale
Dont j'ai oublié l'adresse
À Los Angeles

Cent vingt mille tonnes de pétrole brut
Cent vingt mille tonnes
Chœurs – Dans le Torrey Canyon
Le Torrey Canyon

Lui – Aux Bermudes
À trente degrés d'latitude
Se tient la Barracuda Tan-
Ker's Corporation
Son patron
M'a donné en location
À l'Union Oil Company
De Californie

Cent vingt mille tonnes de pétrole brut
Cent vingt mille tonnes
Chœurs – Dans le Torrey Canyon
Le Torrey Canyon

Lui – Si je bats
Pavillon du Liberia
Le captain et les marins
Sont tous italiens
Le mazout
Dont on m'a rempli les soutes
C'est celui du Consortium
British Petroleum

One hundred twenty thousand tons you crude brute
One hundred twenty thousand tons
CHORISTS – In the Torrey Canyon
The Torrey Canyon
The Torrey Canyon
The Torrey Canyon
The Torrey Canyon
The Torrey Canyon
The Torrey Canyon

Cent vingt mille tonnes espèce de brute
Cent vingt mille tonnes
Chœurs – Dans le Torrey Canyon
Le Torrey Canyon
Le Torrey Canyon
Le Torrey Canyon
Le Torrey Canyon
Le Torrey Canyon
Le Torrey Canyon

Paroles et musique Serge Gainsbourg
© Warner Chappell Music France/Melody Nelson Publishing

FORD MUSTANG [1968]

The first Ford Mustang came out in 1964. Upon hearing of it for the first time, Gainsbourg jotted down the model name on a piece of paper that also contained other future song titles.* It took until 1968, but the iconic model was eventually immortalized in one of Serge's tracks.

HIM – We kiss each other... HER – ALL OVER
HIM – In a... HER – FORD MUSTANG
HIM – And... HER – BANG!
HIM – We swerve around the plane trees
HER – MUS-... HIM – to the left
HER – TANG... HIM – to the right
Back to the left
Back to the right

HIM – Wiper blades, a pack of... HER – KOOLS
HIM – A... HER – BADGE... HIM – upon which is written...
    HER – KEEP COOL
HIM – A chocolate bar
A... HER – COCA-COLA

Chorus

HIM – A bottle of... HER – FLUID MAKE-UP[67]
HIM – A... HER – FLASH[68]... HIM – a... HER – BROWNING[69]...
    HIM – and a... HER – PICK-UP[70]
HIM – A volume of poetry by... HER – EDGAR POE[71]
HIM – A Zippo... HER – LIGHTER

Chorus

HIM – A Superman... HER – ISSUE
HIM – A bolt off... HER – A PACO RABANNE[72]

---

67 "Fluid make-up" is in English in the original lyrics. As the name suggests, it is a cosmetic product.

68 This most likely refers to a flashgun (camera accessory).

69 The Browning firearms company was founded in 1927. As an aside, Clyde Barrow's weapon of choice was known to be the M1918 Browning Automatic Rifle. Gainsbourg may have discovered this while writing *Bonnie and Clyde* [1967] and decided to include a reference in this song.

70 French slang for "record player".

71 Gainsbourg drew from Poe's *The Raven* when writing *Initials BB* [1967].

72 Paco Rabanne (born 1934) is a Spanish haute-couture fashion designer. He was particularly influential on the French fashion scene in the 1960's. His metal-plate, studded dresses were extremely popular at the time and likely constitute the origin of the "bolt" reference (which if literally translated would actually read "nut").

FORD MUSTANG

LUI – **On s'fait des…** ELLE – LANGUES
LUI – **En…** ELLE – FORD MUSTANG
LUI – **Et…** ELLE – BANG !
LUI – **On embrasse les platanes**
ELLE – MUS-… LUI – **à gauche**
ELLE – TANG… LUI – **à droite**
Et à gauche
À droite

LUI – Un essuie-glace, un paquet d'… ELLE – KOOL
LUI – Un… ELLE – BADGE… LUI – avec inscrit dessus…
    ELLE – KEEP COOL
LUI – Une barre de chocolat
Un… ELLE – COCA-COLA

Refrain

LUI – Une bouteille de… ELLE – FLUID MAKE-UP
LUI – Un… ELLE – FLASH… LUI – un… ELLE – BROWNING…
    LUI – et un… ELLE – PICK-UP
LUI – Un recueil… ELLE – D'EDGAR POE
LUI – Un briquet… ELLE – ZIPPO

Refrain

LUI – Un numéro de… ELLE – SUPERMAN
LUI – Un écrou de chez… ELLE – PACO RABANNE

HIM – A photo of… HER – MARILYN[73]
HIM – A bottle of… HER – ASPIRIN

HIM – We kiss each other… HER – ALL OVER
HIM – In a… HER – FORD MUSTANG
HIM – And… HER – BANG!
HIM – We swerve around the sycamores
HER – MUS-… HIM – to the left
HER – TANG… HIM – to the right[74]

---

73 Marilyn Monroe had died a few years earlier, in 1962.

74 By their absence, the last two lines of the chorus symbolize the car crash that claimed the couple's lives.**

LUI – Une photo d'… ELLE – MARILYN
LUI – Un tube… ELLE – D'ASPIRINE

LUI – On s'fait des… ELLE – LANGUES
LUI – En… ELLE – FORD MUSTANG
LUI – Et… ELLE – BANG
LUI – On embrasse les platanes
ELLE – MUS-… LUI – à gauche
ELLE – TANG… LUI – à droite

Paroles et musique Serge Gainsbourg
© Warner Chappell Music France/Melody Nelson Publishing

HOLD-UP [1967]

Sadomasochism is the guest of honor in this song.

I've come to rob you of[75]
One hundred million kisses
One hundred million kisses
In small burns
In small bites
In small denominations[76]

CHORISTS - It's a hold-up
HIM – Oh yeah, it's a hold-up
CHORISTS - A hold-up
HIM - A hold-up
CHORISTS - A hold-up
HIM - A hold-up
CHORISTS - A hold-up

If you won't hand them over to me
I'll be forced to tie you up
Leaving on your wrists
Small burns
Small bites
Small cuts

CHORISTS - It's a hold-up
HIM – Yep, it's a hold-up
CHORISTS - A hold-up
HIM - A hold-up
CHORISTS - A hold-up
HIM - A hold-up
CHORISTS - A hold-up

Now that I have your kisses
Nothing's left for me to do but leave
And for you to do but forget
Your small burns
Your small bites
Your small cuts

---

75   "I've come to …" foreshadows 1973's classic *Je suis venu te dire que je m'en vais* (*I've Come to Tell You that I'm Leaving*).

76   The French word "coupure" can mean either "denomination" or "cut" depending on the context.

HOLD-UP

Lui – Je suis venu pour te voler
Cent millions de baisers
Cent millions de baisers
En petites brûlures
En petites morsures
En petites coupures

Chœurs – C'est un hold-up
Lui – Eh ! ouais, c'est un hold-up
Chœurs – Un hold-up
Lui – Un hold-up
Chœurs – Un hold-up
Lui – Un hold-up
Chœurs – Un hold-up

Lui – Si tu ne veux pas m'les donner
J'serai forcé de t'attacher
Et ça t'fera aux poignets
Des petites brûlures
Des petites morsures
Des petites coupures

Chœurs – C'est un hold-up
Lui – Ouais, c'est un hold-up
Chœurs – Un hold-up
Lui – Un hold-up
Chœurs – Un hold-up
Lui – Un hold-up
Chœurs – Un hold-up

Lui – Maintenant que j'ai tes baisers
Il m'reste plus qu'à m'tailler
Et toi à oublier
Ces petites brûlures
Ces petites morsures
Ces petites coupures

CHORISTS - It's a hold-up
HIM – Yep, it's a hold-up
CHORISTS - A hold-up
HIM - A hold-up
CHORISTS - A hold-up
HIM - A hold-up
CHORISTS - A hold-up
HIM - A hold-up
CHORISTS - A hold-up
HIM - A hold-up
CHORISTS - A hold-up

Chœurs – **C'est un hold-up**
Lui – **Ouais, c'est un hold-up**
Chœurs – **Un hold-up**
Lui – **Un hold-up**
Chœurs – **Un hold-up**
Lui – **Un hold-up**
Chœurs – **Un hold-up**
Lui – **Un hold-up**
Chœurs – **Un hold-up**
Lui – **Un hold-up**
Chœurs – **Un hold-up**

Paroles et musique Serge Gainsbourg
© Sidonie/Melody Nelson Publishing

JE T'AIME MOI NON PLUS —
SERGE MEETS JANE

Serge and Jane Birkin first met on the set of Pierre Grimblat's film *Slogan* in May of 1968. Paris was awash in student violence and civil unrest as the chaotic events of *mai 68* unfolded. Not only was 21-year-old Jane playing in a foreign film amidst some of the worst turmoil the French capital had ever seen, her co-star was taking great pleasure in ignoring her (Gainsbourg was disappointed that American model Marisa Berenson was not starring alongside him). Not surprisingly, Jane left the set in tears.*

A conversation recounted by Jane's brother, Andrew Birkin, for the British newspaper *The Telegraph* is particularly telling. An excerpt from his 2013 piece:

"Jane was also in Paris [...] making a low-budget French film about which she complained bitterly.

'He's horrible!'

'Who?'

'Serge Bourguignon! The man in the film with me. He's meant to be my lover but he's so arrogant and snobbish and he absolutely despises me!'"

In order to smooth over the situation, Grimblat made a reservation for the three of them at *Maxim's,* perhaps the most famous restaurant in the world at the time. Conveniently, Grimblat never showed.* After dinner, Serge took Jane out for a night of drinking at his favorite clubs. The Pigalle establishment *Madame Arthur's,* a transvestite cabaret where Serge's father had worked as a pianist, made the cut that night, as did *New Jimmy's,* a Régine-owned Montparnasse club.[77]

Serge and Jane ended up at the Hilton hotel, where a droll (or perhaps formidably inept) concierge asked Serge if he would like "the usual, room 642?" Nothing happened between the couple, as Serge quickly proceeded to pass out on the bed.[78] Just like that, a formidable decade-long romance was born.

---

77 Gainsbourg, Verlant, **2000**, Albin Michel.
78 Gainsbourg, Verlant, **2000**, Albin Michel.

Serge and Jane Birkin at the premiere of Slogan *on August 28, 1969. Director Pierre Grimblat (wearing a tie) is in the background.*

Photo by Yves Le Roux

LA CHANSON DE SLOGAN — THE SLOGAN SONG [1969]

With unsettling accuracy, this song seems to predict the end of the passionate relationship Serge and Jane would maintain until 1980, when Jane broke things off with the increasingly erratic, aggressive, and alcohol-abusing Serge.

> HER – You are weak, you are deceitful, you are crazy
> You are cold, you are fake, you don't care
> HIM – Évelyne, I beg you, Évelyne, don't say that
> Évelyne, you loved me, believe me
>
> HER – You are vile, you are spineless, you are vain
> You are old, you are hollow, you are nothing
> HIM – Évelyne, you're unfair, Évelyne, you are wrong
> Évelyne, you see, you still love me
>
> HER – You are weak, you are deceitful, you are crazy
> You are cold, you are fake, you don't care
> HIM – Évelyne, you're unfair, Évelyne, you are wrong
> Évelyne, you see, you still love me

LA CHANSON DE SLOGAN

ELLE – Tu es faible, tu es fourbe, tu es fou
Tu es froid, tu es faux, tu t'en fous
LUI – Évelyne, je t'en prie, Évelyne, dis pas ça
Évelyne, tu m'as aimé, crois-moi

ELLE – Tu es vil, tu es veule, tu es vain
Tu es vieux, tu es vide, tu n'es rien
LUI – Évelyne, tu es injuste, Évelyne, tu as tort
Évelyne, tu vois, tu m'aimes encore

ELLE – Tu es faible, tu es fourbe, tu es fou
Tu es froid, tu es faux, tu t'en fous
LUI – Évelyne, tu es injuste, Évelyne, tu as tort
Évelyne, tu vois, tu m'aimes encore

Paroles Serge Gainsbourg
Musique Serge Gainsbourg et Jean-Claude Vannier
© Manèges/Semi/Warner Chappell Music France/Melody Nelson
    Publishing/Jean-Claude Vannier

JE T'AIME MOI NON PLUS — I LOVE YOU ME NEITHER [1967]

The song Gainsbourg is known for the world over. It was first recorded with Brigitte Bardot in 1967, although that version was not released until 1986.** Despite a promise made to Bardot never to release the song (she was married at the time of their relationship), Gainsbourg re-recorded it in 1969 with an initially reticent Jane Birkin.* Birkin sang an octave higher than Bardot, injected heavier doses of deep breathing, and the song went on to become a smash hit despite clerical and government opposition.

Je t'aime moi non plus was the first French song to hit #1 in the UK, BBC censorship notwithstanding. The official newspaper of the Vatican called on citizens to boycott this "obscenity" and managed to have pressing stopped in Italy. Spain, Portugal, Brazil, Sweden and Holland followed suit.*

After filming *Les chemins de Katmandou (Pleasure Pit)* in Nepal, Jane and Serge headed home to savor the success of *Je t'aime moi non plus* from Gainsbourg's newly acquired property in Paris' 6th arrondissement, on the rue de Verneuil. Gainsbourg would live at number 5 *bis* on this street for the rest of his life.

> HER – I love you, I love you
> Oh! yes, I love you
> HIM – Me neither
> HER – Oh! my love
> HIM – Like the wavering wave
> I come, I come and I go[79]
> Between your loins
> I come and I go
> Between your loins
> And I
> Hold
> Back
>
> HER – I love you, I love you
> Oh! yes, I love you
> HIM – Me neither
> HER – Oh! my love
> You are the wave to my naked island
> You come, you come and you go
> Between my loins
> You come and you go
> Between my loins
> And I
> Join
> You

---

79 The original lyrics, translated word-for-word, would have yielded: "I go, I go and I come". Indeed, in French, the correct order for the idiom is "to go and come", not "to come and go". The French version is evidently a better fit when taking innuendo into account.

JE T'AIME MOI NON PLUS

ELLE – Je t'aime, je t'aime
Oh ! oui, je t'aime
LUI – Moi non plus
ELLE – Oh ! mon amour
LUI – Comme la vague irrésolue
Je vais, je vais et je viens
Entre tes reins
Je vais et je viens
Entre tes reins
Et je
Me re-
Tiens

ELLE – Je t'aime, je t'aime
Oh ! oui, je t'aime
LUI – Moi non plus
ELLE – Oh ! mon amour
Tu es la vague, moi l'île nue
Tu vas, tu vas et tu viens
Entre mes reins
Tu vas et tu viens
Entre mes reins
Et je
Te re-
Joins

I love you, I love you
Oh! yes, I love you
HIM – Me neither
HER – Oh my love
HIM – Like the wavering wave
I come, I come and I go
Between your loins
I come and I go
Between your loins
And I
Hold
Back

HER – You come, you come and you go
Between my loins
You come and you go
Between my loins
And I
Join
You

I love you, I love you
Oh! yes, I love you
HIM – Me neither
HER – Oh! my love
HIM – Sex is a dead end[80]
I come, I come and I go
Between your loins
I come and I go
I hold back
HER – No, it's time
For you
To come!

---

80 Literally translated, the verse reads: "Physical love is a dead end".

Je t'aime, je t'aime
Oh ! oui, je t'aime
LUI – Moi non plus
ELLE – Oh ! mon amour
LUI – Comme la vague irrésolue
Je vais, je vais et je viens
Entre tes reins
Je vais et je viens
Entre tes reins
Et je
Me re-
Tiens

ELLE – Tu vas, tu vas et tu viens
Entre mes reins
Tu vas et tu viens
Entre mes reins
Et je
Te re-
Joins

Je t'aime, je t'aime
Oh ! oui, je t'aime
LUI – Moi non plus
ELLE – Oh ! mon amour
LUI – L'amour physique est sans issue
Je vais, je vais et je viens
Entre tes reins
Je vais et je viens
Je me retiens
ELLE – Non, main-
Tenant
Viens !

Paroles et musique Serge Gainsbourg
© Melody Nelson Publishing

L'ANAMOUR — ANAMOUR [1968]

One of Gainsbourg's most beautiful songs. Everything about it is peculiar, from the inexplicable lyrics to the neologism on which they are founded ("amour" means "love" in French, and "ana" is a common prefix that can mean anything from "up" to "again" to "backward"). The listening experience is singularly moving.

Not a single Boeing on my flight path
Not a single boat visible from my deck chair
In vain I search for the right door
In vain I search for the word exit

For the transistors I sing
The strange story
Of my transitory anamours
Of a Sleeping Beauty

I love you and I fear
I may lose my way
And I sow seeds
Of poppy on the cobblestones
Of anamour

You know, those photos of Asia
That I took at 200 ASA[81]
Now that you're not here
Their bright colors have faded

I thought I'd heard the blades
Of a four-engined jet but alas
It's a ceiling fan tossing about
In the police station sky[82]

Chorus x3

81 This refers to a method developed by the American Standards Association (ASA) for measuring film speed. The ASA is now the American National Standards Institute (ANSI).
82 A similar parallel can later be found in the opening scene of Francis Ford Coppola's 1979 epic *Apocalypse Now*: the blades of a helicopter's rotor gradually give way to those of a ceiling fan as the audience joins Captain Willard in his Saigon hotel room.

L'ANAMOUR

Aucun Boeing sur mon transit
Aucun bateau sous mon transat
Je cherche en vain la porte exacte
Je cherche en vain le mot exit

Je chante pour les transistors
Le récit de l'étrange histoire
De mes anamours transitoires
De Belle au Bois Dormant qui dort

Je t'aime et je crains
De m'égarer
Et je sème des grains
De pavot sur les pavés
De l'anamour

Tu sais, ces photos de l'Asie
Que j'ai prises à deux cents ASA
Maintenant que tu n'es pas là
Leurs couleurs vives ont pâli

J'ai cru entendre les hélices
D'un quadrimoteur mais hélas
C'est un ventilateur qui passe
Au ciel du poste de police

Refrain trissé

Paroles et musique Serge Gainsbourg
© 1968 by Melody Nelson Publishing/Editions & Productions Sidonie

SOIXANTE-NEUF ANNÉE EROTIQUE — SIXTY-NINE EROTIC YEAR [1969]

Gainsbourg's classic homage to Jane Birkin, in whom he found true love.

HIM - Gainsbourg and his Gainsborough[83]
Took the ferry boat
From their bed through the porthole
They gaze at the coast

They're in love and the crossing
Will last an entire year
They will counter evil spells
Well into seventy[84]

HER – Soixante-neuf
Année érotique
Soixante-neuf
Année érotique[85]

HIM – Gainsbourg and his Gainsborough
Are headed to Paris
They've left behind
The Thames and Chelsea[86]

They're in love and the crossing
Will last an entire year
And may the Gods bless them
Well into seventy

Chorus

HIM – They're in love and the crossing
Will last an entire year
He'll forgive her whimsy
Well into seventy

Chorus

---

83 Thomas Gainsborough (1727-1788) was an English portrait and landscape painter. Clearly chosen due to the similarity between his last name and Gainsbourg's, the latter substitutes the painter for Jane Birkin. In doing so, Gainsbourg intimates that Birkin is as lovely as a Gainsborough canvas, while also highlighting his girlfriend's Englishness at a time when being a Brit in France was very much *en vogue*.** In a 2008 interview given to the *Daily Mail*, Birkin explains: *"I was a Brit [in Paris] at the perfect time. It was the British renaissance. David Bailey. Mini-skirts. The King's Road."*

84 Abbreviation for the year 1970.

85 Your translator has made a conscious decision to keep the chorus of this song in French. The English translation leaves much to be desired; besides, the chorus is already somewhat anglicized by Jane Birkin's accent.

86 Birkin's parents lived in Chelsea, a residential London neighborhood.**

SOIXANTE-NEUF ANNÉE ÉROTIQUE

Lui – Gainsbourg et son Gainsborough
Ont pris le ferry-boat
De leur lit par le hublot
Ils regardent la côte

Ils s'aiment et la traversée
Durera toute une année
Ils vaincront les maléfices
Jusqu'en soixante-dix

Elle – Soixante-neuf
Année érotique
Soixante-neuf
Année érotique

Lui – Gainsbourg et son Gainsborough
Vont rejoindre Paris
Ils ont laissé derrière eux
La Tamise et Chelsea

Ils s'aiment et la traversée
Durera toute une année
Et que les Dieux les bénissent
Jusqu'en soixante-dix

Refrain

Lui – Ils s'aiment et la traversée
Durera toute une année
Il pardonnera ses caprices
Jusqu'en soixante-dix

Refrain

Paroles et musique Serge Gainsbourg
© Warner Chappell Music France/Melody Nelson Publishing

ÉLISA [1969]

This song's melody was originally composed for the soundtrack of Jacques Rouffio's 1967 film *L'horizon*. Two years later, when Gainsbourg tailored lyrics to the melody in a tribute to Jane Birkin, another classic was born.

Élisa, Élisa
Élisa, throw your arms around my neck[87]
Élisa, Élisa,
Élisa, check me for lice

Dig your nails nice and deep
And your delicate fingers
Into the jungle[88]
That is my hair, Lisa

Élisa, Élisa
Élisa, throw your arms around my neck
Élisa, Élisa,
Élisa, check me for lice

Make me a few curls
And a part down the middle
Between the two of us we've lived
Thirteen, fourteen years

Élisa, Élisa
Élisa, who cares about ither people
Élisa, Élisa,
Élisa, nobody but you, me, us

You're twenty, I'm forty[89]
If you believe
This torments me
Ah! No, really, Lisa[90]

---

87 Gainsbourg uses the expression "saute-moi au cou", which, literally translated, means "jump up on my neck". The French generally understand it to mean "wrap your arms around my neck and your legs around my waist".

88 Although clearly meaning "jungle", Gainsbourg pronounces the word as though it were spelled "jongle". The same pronunciation can later be found in *Cargo culte* [1971], *King Kong* [1972], *Bambou* [1981] and *Lost song* [1987].**

89 In 1969, Birkin was 23 and Gainsbourg was 41.

90 Gainsbourg's tone when uttering this line is one of gentle, nearly paternal, assertiveness. He seems to say: "See, sweetheart, it's like this." One can almost hear Humbert Humbert addressing his beloved Lola in this verse.

ÉLISA

Élisa, Élisa
Élisa, saute-moi au cou
Élisa, Élisa
Élisa, cherche-moi des poux

Enfonce bien tes ongles
Et tes doigts délicats
Dans la jungle
De mes cheveux, Lisa

Élisa, Élisa
Élisa, saute-moi au cou
Élisa, Élisa
Élisa, cherche-moi des poux

Fais-moi quelques anglaises
Et la raie au milieu
On a treize
Quatorze ans à nous deux

Élisa, Élisa
Élisa, les autres on s'en fout
Élisa, Élisa
Élisa, rien que toi, moi, nous

Tes vingt ans, mes quarante
Si tu crois que cela
Me tourmente
Ah ! non, vraiment, Lisa

Élisa, Élisa
Élisa, throw your arms around my neck
Élisa, Élisa,
Élisa, check me for lice

Dig your nails nice and deep
And your delicate fingers
Into the jungle
That is my hair, Lisa

Élisa, Élisa
Élisa, saute-moi au cou
Élisa, Élisa
Élisa, cherche-moi des poux

Enfonce bien tes ongles
Et tes doigts délicats
Dans la jongle
De mes cheveux, Lisa

Paroles Serge Gainsbourg
Musique Serge Gainsbourg et Michel Colombier

© 1969 by Editions et Productions Sidonie & Melody Nelson Publishing

CANNABIS [1970]

Gainsbourg's voice is a thing to behold on this piece, which stands out as the crown jewel of the soundtrack he wrote for Pierre Koralnik's 1970 film *Cannabis*, co-starring himself and Jane Birkin. The film's central themes – drugs, love, and death – all figure prominently in this song.

Koralnik and Gainsbourg had worked together before, most notably on *Anna*[91] three years prior.

Death
Has the face of a little girl
Who sees right through me
Her body
Fashioned for the subtleties of love
Will forever captivate me

**She calls me by my name
And suddenly I lose my mind
Is it an evil spell
Or the subtle effect of cannabis**

Chorus

Death
Arms and legs spreading under me
Has wrapped herself around me
Her body
Manages to extract from mine groans of pleasure
And one final sigh

---

91 For more on this film, see introductory notes to the chapter titled *Between Life and Love: Anna, The Musical.*

CANNABIS

La mort
A pour moi le visage d'une enfant
Au regard transparent
Son corps
Habile au raffinement de l'amour
Me prendra pour toujours

Elle m'appelle par mon nom
Quand soudain je perds la raison
Est-ce un maléfice
Ou l'effet subtil du cannabis

Refrain

La mort
Ouvrant sous moi ses jambes et ses bras
S'est refermée sur moi
Son corps
M'arrache enfin les râles du plaisir
Et mon dernier soupir

Paroles Serge Gainsbourg
Musique Serge Gainsbourg et Jean-Claude Vannier
© Editions & Productions Sidonie

LA NOYÉE — THE DROWNED WOMAN [1971]

The theme of this song is taken from Arthur Rimbaud's poem *Ophélie*.* Rimbaud (1854-1891) was a genius, and is often considered the best French poet to have ever lived. This distinction is made all the more impressive by the fact that he completed most of his works as a teenager, having chosen to stop writing poetry altogether at twenty years of age in favor of a nomadic, globe-trotting existence. He first came to Paris under the protection of Paul Verlaine (see *Je suis venu te dire que je m'en vais*) with whom he maintained a passionate, destructive relationship for a time. Things between the two came to a head in 1873 when Verlaine, in a drunken stupor, shot Rimbaud in Brussels. Rimbaud was only slightly wounded. Verlaine would serve two years in prison, and the pair would meet only once more after the incident.

This song was meant to be sung by Yves Montand, an acclaimed French vocalist. However Montand never recorded it, perhaps fearing the lyrics would be misconstrued because his wife, the actress Simone Signoret, suffered from a fairly public drinking problem. Montand had previously refused to record *Le Poinçonneur des Lilas* in 1958.*

The song appeared in the soundtrack of Abraham Polonsky's 1971 film *Romance of a Horsethief*.*

Away you drift
On the river of memory
As I run on the bank
Crying for you to come back
But slowly you become more distant
And in my desperate chase
Little by little I recover
Some of the ground lost to you

At times you sink
Into the moving depths
At others, brushing against the reeds
You hesitate and wait for me
Hiding your face
In your hiked up[92] dress
For fear of being disfigured
By shame and regrets

You're nothing now but an empty shell
A dead bitch in the current
But I remain your slave
And dive into the stream
When memory ends

---

92 Melody Nelson, Gainsbourg's famous Lolita character, also has a "hiked up" skirt when the narrator first meets her following the car accident. The same French adjective ("retroussée") is used in both instances. See *Melody* [1971].

LA NOYÉE

Tu t'en vas à la dérive
Sur la rivière du souvenir
Et moi courant sur la rive
Je te crie de revenir
Mais lentement tu t'éloignes
Et dans ma course éperdue
Peu à peu je te regagne
Un peu du terrain perdu

De temps en temps tu t'enfonces
Dans le liquide mouvant
Ou bien frôlant quelques ronces
Tu hésites et tu m'attends
En te cachant la figure
Dans ta robe retroussée
De peur que n'te défigurent
Et la honte et les regrets

Tu n'es plus qu'une pauvre épave
Chienne crevée au fil de l'eau
Mais je reste ton esclave
Et plonge dans le ruisseau
Quand le souvenir s'arrête

And a purifying ocean[93]
Fracturing our hearts and minds
Forever reunites us

---

93 There is no term for "oubli" in English, a noun that literally means the opposite of "memory".

Et l'océan de l'oubli
Brisant nos cœurs et nos têtes
À jamais nous réunit

HISTOIRE DE MELODY NELSON

In March of 1971, Gainsbourg released his first concept album, titled *Histoire de Melody Nelson (The Story of Melody Nelson)*. The record was praised by critics upon release, but sold poorly. It has since gained cult status and is now considered to be one of Gainsbourg's masterpieces.

Symphonic music provides the bass-heavy backdrop for the story of a man who drives his Rolls-Royce into a bicycle-riding young girl, only to ultimately seduce her, take her virginity, and lose her to a plane crash. Jane Birkin delivers the dreamy, ethereal female vocals.

MELODY [1971]

Melody tells the story of the first encounter between the eponymous Lolita and the narrator.

HIM – *The Rolls*[94] *wings grazed the traffic posts*
And despite my best intentions, I found myself lost
As we arrived, the Rolls and I, in a dangerous
Neighborhood, an isolated place

***

HIM – *Down there, on the hood of the nineteen ten*
Silver Ghost, a scout takes up position
It's the radiator's silver Venus[95]
A billowing dress spiriting her to the outpost

Haughty, disdainful, as the radio's blare
Drowns out the silence of the motor
She sets her sights on the horizon and, mind elsewhere
Seems utterly oblivious to the curbs I run into

Blithely, she harnesses the power of twenty-six horses
Directing them through side streets and blind alleys
Along which loitering is forbidden

Princess of darkness, cursed archangel
A modern Amazon nicknamed
"Spirit of Ecstasy" by her sculptor

***

HIM – *And so I goofed off, until I lost*
Control of the Rolls. I was driving slowly
When my car veered off course, and a hard collision
Suddenly snapped me out of my reverie. Shit.

I caught sight of a bike tire
Freewheeling in front of me
And like a tenuously balanced doll
Skirt hiked up over her white pants

---

94 Despite not having a driver's license, Serge had just bought himself a Rolls Royce with the fifty thousand francs earned on the set of Polonsky's *Romance of a Horsethief* – see *La Noyée* [1971].

95 The next few stanzas reference the hood ornament found on all Rolls-Royce vehicles. Known as the "Spirit of Ecstasy", it depicts a forward-leaning woman, arms outstretched with cloth billowing behind her.

MELODY

Lui – *Les ailes de la Rolls effleuraient des pylônes*
Quand, m'étant malgré moi égaré
Nous arrivâmes, ma Rolls et moi, dans une zone
Dangereuse, un endroit isolé

***

Lui – *Là-bas, sur le capot de cette Silver Ghost*
De dix-neuf cent dix, s'avance en éclaireur
La Vénus d'argent du radiateur
Dont les voiles légers volent aux avant-postes

Hautaine, dédaigneuse, tandis qu'hurle le poste
De radio couvrant le silence du moteur
Elle fixe l'horizon et, l'esprit ailleurs
Semble tout ignorer des trottoirs que j'accoste

Ruelles, culs-de-sac aux stationnements
Interdits par la loi, le cœur indifférent
Elle tient le mors de mes vingt-six chevaux vapeur

Princesse des ténèbres, archange maudit
Amazone modern style que le sculpteur
En anglais, surnomma "Spirit of Ecstasy"

***

Lui – *Ainsi je déconnais, avant que je ne perde*
Le contrôle de la Rolls. J'avançais lentement
Ma voiture dériva, et un heurt violent
Me tira soudain de ma rêverie. Merde

J'aperçus une roue de vélo à l'avant
Qui continuait de tourner en roue libre
Et comme une poupée, qui perdait l'équilibre
La jupe retroussée sur ses pantalons blancs

***

HIM – *What's your name*
HER – *Melody*
HIM – *Melody what*
HER – *Melody Nelson*

***

HIM – *Melody Nelson has red hair*
And that's its natural color

***

LUI – *Tu t'appelles comment*
ELLE – *Melody*
LUI – *Melody comment*
ELLE – *Melody Nelson*

***

L**UI** – *Melody Nelson a les cheveux rouges*
Et c'est leur couleur naturelle

Paroles et musique Serge Gainsbourg
© Editions & Productions Sidonie/Warner Chappell Music France/
  Melody Nelson Publishing

BALLADE DE MELODY NELSON — THE BALLAD OF MELODY NELSON [1971]

The listener develops a clearer picture of Melody's tender age and carefree innocence.

> HIM – This is the story of... HER – Melody Nelson
> HIM – Who's been embraced by no one
> Save for me
> You seem skeptical
> But it's the truth
>
> She had so much love, that poor... HER – Melody Nelson
> HIM – Yeah, she had tons of it
> But her days were numbered
> Fourteen autumns
> And fifteen summers
>
> She had a wild streak that... HER – Melody Nelson
> HIM – Such an adorable little tomboy
> And such a delicious child
> Whom I knew only
> For an instant
>
> Oh! My Melody, my... HER – Melody Nelson
> HIM – Such a fucking little fool[96]
> My sanity
> Was contingent upon
> Your existence

---

96 The original lyrics make it clear that the epithet is directed toward Melody, not the narrator.

BALLADE DE MELODY NELSON

Lui – Ça, c'est l'histoire de… Elle – Melody Nelson
Lui – Qu'à part moi-même personne
N'a jamais pris dans ses bras
Ça vous étonne
Mais c'est comme ça

Elle avait d'l'amour, pauvre… Elle – Melody Nelson
Lui – Ouais, elle en avait des tonnes
Mais ses jours étaient comptés
Quatorze automnes
Et quinze étés

Un p'tit animal que cette… Elle – Melody Nelson
Lui – Une adorable garçonne
Et si délicieuse enfant
Que je n'ai con-
Nue qu'un instant

Oh ! Ma Melody, ma… Elle – Melody Nelson
Lui – Aimable petite conne
Tu étais la condition
Sine qua non
De ma raison

Paroles Serge Gainsbourg
Musique Jean-Claude Vannier

VALSE DE MELODY — MELODY'S WALTZ [1971]

The chorus of this song may be a subtle reference to Melody's virginity.*

Sunlight is fleeting
As is happiness
Love loses its way
Along the path of life

Sunlight is fleeting
As is happiness
But Melody's arms
Set everything in motion

The labyrinth's fortifications
Lay ajar and
Keep watch over infinity

Sunlight is fleeting
As is happiness
But Melody's arms
Set everything in motion

Chorus

VALSE DE MELODY

Le soleil est rare
Et le bonheur aussi
L'amour s'égare
Au long de la vie

Le soleil est rare
Et le bonheur aussi
Mais tout bouge
Au bras de Melody

Les murs d'enceinte
Du labyrinthe
S'entrouvrent sur l'infini

Le soleil est rare
Et le bonheur aussi
Mais tout bouge
Au bras de Melody

Refrain

Paroles et musique de Serge Gainsbourg
© Warner Chappell Music France/Editions & Productions Sidonie/
    Melody Nelson Publishing

AH! MELODY [1971]

Ah! Melody relates the first sexual encounter between the narrator and Melody Nelson, who is just discovering physical love. Their erotic foreplay has the narrator questioning whether Melody is truly a virgin.

> **Ah! Melody**
> **You'll have made me**
> **Do such stupid things**
> **Giddy up, giddy up and whoa**
> **As you ride my back**
>
> Oh! Melody
> You know not what love is
> You told me as much
> But is there truth to all you say
>
> **Chorus**
>
> Oh! Melody
> If you lied to me, I'll fall
> Ill over it[97]
> I don't know what I'll do to you

---

97   This is not the only time Gainsbourg has a protagonist "fall ill" over one of his Lolita muses: he will do so again with Marilou in 1976 (*Marilou sous la neige*).

AH ! MELODY

Ah ! Melody
Tu m'en auras fait fai-
Re, des conneries
Hue, hue et ho
À dada sur mon dos

Oh ! Melody
L'amour tu n'sais pas ce que c'est
Tu me l'as dit
Mais tout c'que tu dis est-il vrai

Refrain

Oh ! Melody
Si tu m'as menti, j'en ferai
Une maladie
Je n'sais pas c'que je te ferai

Paroles Serge Gainsbourg
Musique Jean Claude Vannier
© Editions et Productions Sidonie/Warner Chappell Music France/
     Melody Nelson Publishing/Jean-Claude Vannier

L'HÔTEL PARTICULIER — THE HÔTEL PARTICULIER[98] [1971]

The climax of the album. The narrator relieves Melody of her innocence in an ornate mansion (or bordello?) as the music takes on epic proportions.

At number fifty-six, -seven, -eight, no matter
On X Street, if you rap on the door
First one knock, then three more, they let you in
Alone or sometimes even in good company

Without saying a word, a maid leads the way
Through endless hallways and stairwells
Dotted with golden cherubs and baroque bronzes
Of Aphrodite[99] and Salome[100]

If it's vacant, request number forty-four
It's the one they've dubbed Cleopatra's room
The one where Negroes carrying torches
Double as rococo bedposts

Amidst these nude slaves carved into the ebony
All of them mute witnesses to the scene
While a ceiling mirror reflects us from above
Slowly, I wrap my arms around Melody

Melody
Melody

---

98   The French "hôtel particulier" is rather untranslatable. The term is used when referring to a grand and urban private residence, usually a house on several floors.

99   In Greek mythology, Aphrodite is the goddess of love, beauty, sexual pleasure, and procreation. Her Roman equivalent is Venus.

100   Salome (c. AD 14 – between 62 and 71) was the daughter of Herod II and Herodias. She has become somewhat of a symbol for pernicious female seductiveness.

L'HÔTEL PARTICULIER

Au cinquante-six, sept, huit, peu importe
De la rue X, si vous frappez à la porte
D'abord un coup, puis trois autres, on vous laisse entrer
Seul et parfois même accompagné

Une servante, sans vous dire un mot, vous précède
Des escaliers, des couloirs sans fin se succèdent
Décorés de bronzes baroques, d'anges dorés
D'Aphrodites et de Salomés

S'il est libre, dites que vous voulez le quarante-quatre
C'est la chambre qu'ils appellent ici de Cléopâtre
Dont les colonnes du lit de style rococo
Sont des nègres portant des flambeaux

Entre ces esclaves nus taillés dans l'ébène
Qui seront les témoins muets de cette scène
Tandis que là-haut un miroir nous réfléchit
Lentement, j'enlace Melody

Melody
Melody

EN MELODY — IN MELODY [1971]

This quasi-instrumental sequence serves as a transition between the lovers' passionate stay at the *hôtel particulier* and the tragedy that ensues.*

> *Melody wanted to see the skies of Sunderland[101] again*
> *She took the seven oh seven[102], the red-eye cargo plane*
> *But the autopilot at the aircraft's controls*
> *Committed an error that proved fatal to Melody*

---

101 Sunderland is a British city on the outskirts of Newcastle upon Tyne.
102 Boeing's 707 model is referenced here.

EN MELODY

Melody voulut revoir le ciel de Sunderland
Elle prit le sept cent sept, l'avion cargo de nuit
Mais le pilote automatique aux commandes
De l'appareil fit une erreur fatale à Melody

Paroles Serge Gainsbourg
Musique Serge Gainsbourg et Jean-Claude Vannier
© Bagatelle/Warner Chappell Music France/Melody Nelson Publishing/
  Jean-Claude Vannier

CARGO CULTE – CARGO CULT [1971]

A cargo cult is "any of the religious movements, chiefly in Melanesia[103] in the late 19th and early 20th century, based on the observation by local residents of the delivery of exotic supplies by ship and aircraft to colonial officials. The cults exhibited the expectation of a new age of blessing and prosperity to be initiated by the arrival of a special 'cargo' of goods from supernatural sources."[104]

Richard Feynman[105] popularized the use of the term in his 1974 commencement address at Caltech, using it to denounce shoddy scientific work: "In the South Seas there is a Cargo Cult of people. During the war they saw airplanes land with lots of good materials, and they want the same thing to happen now. So they've arranged to make things like runways, to put fires along the sides of the runways, to make a wooden hut for a man to sit in, with two wooden pieces on his head like headphones and bars of bamboo sticking out like antennas – he's the controller – and they wait for the airplanes to land. They're doing everything right. The form is perfect. It looks exactly the way it looked before. But it doesn't work. No airplanes land. So I call these things Cargo Cult science, because they follow all the apparent precepts and forms of scientific investigation, but they're missing something essential, because the planes don't land."

In Gainsbourg's imaginary cargo cult civilization, natives shoot at airplanes with blowpipes in the hopes that one might crash and deliver them its treasures. The narrator also finds himself turning to cargo cult in the hopes that it may lead to Melody's reincarnation.

> HIM – *I've heard tell of sorcerers who summon jets*
> *In the jungles of New Guinea*
> *They scan the horizon, longing for the guineas*
> *That the plane's cargo would fetch*
>
> *During the aircraft's passage over*
> *The coral sea, these perfectly sane creatures*
> *These Guineans, fully expect the skies to deliver*
> *Misfortune to Viscounts and Comets*[106]
>
> *And since their totem has never brought down*
> *Neither Boeings nor even DC-4's*[107]

---

103   A subdivision of Oceania, Melanesia includes among others: Papua New Guinea, Fiji, Vanuatu, and New Caledonia.

104   Britannica Concise Encyclopedia, **2000**.

105   Richard Feynman (1918-1988) was an American theoretical physicist, winner of the Nobel Prize in 1965.

106   The Vickers Viscount and the de Havilland Comet were both British aircraft that made their debuts in the late 1940's. The first generation Comet suffered several well-publicized crashes that were ultimately attributed to design flaws.

107   The Douglas DC-4 is an American airplane that served extensively in World War II and in the Berlin Airlift.

CARGO CULTE

Lui – *Je sais, moi, des sorciers qui invoquent les jets*
Dans la jungle de Nouvelle-Guinée
Et scrutent le zénith, convoitant les guinées
Que leur rapporterait le pillage du fret

Sur la mer de corail au passage de cet
Appareil, ces créatures non dénuées
De raison, ces Papous attendent des nuées
L'avarie du Viscount et celle du Comet

Et comme leur totem n'a jamais pu abattre
À leurs pieds ni Boeing ni même DC quatre

They dream of hijacks and avian encounters

These naïve pirates armed with blowguns
Shoot air at the seas and the planes
Devoting their lives to cargo cult

***

HIM – *Where are you Melody, and does your broken body*
Haunt the siren-inhabited atoll
Or did you stay by the cargo
Clinging to the wreckage as the last alarms fell silent

By the grace of the currents have you reached
The bright coral off the coast of Guinea
Where indigenous sorcerers thrash about in vain
Placing their hopes in shattered planes

Having nothing more to lose and no God to believe in
I, like them, prayed to the night cargo
That it might return my pitiful loves[108] to me

And so I hold out hope for an aerial
Disaster that would to me bring back Melody
That celestially corrupted young girl

***

HIM – *What's your name*
HER – *Melody*
HIM – *Melody what*
HER – *Melody Nelson*

---

108 The original lyrics use the plural form of the word.

Ils rêvent de hijacks et d'accidents d'oiseaux

Ces naufrageurs naïfs armés de sarbacanes
Qui sacrifient ainsi au culte du cargo
En soufflant vers l'azur et les aéroplanes

***

Lui – *Où es-tu Melody, et ton corps disloqué*
Hante-t-il l'archipel que peuplent les sirènes
Ou bien, accrochée au cargo dont la sirène
D'alarme s'est tue, es-tu restée

Au hasard des courants, as-tu déjà touché
Ces lumineux coraux des côtes guinéennes
Où s'agitent en vain ces sorciers indigènes
Qui espèrent encore en des avions brisés

N'ayant plus rien à perdre ni Dieu en qui croire
Afin qu'ils me rendent mes amours dérisoires
Moi, comme eux, j'ai prié les cargos de la nuit

Et je garde cette espérance d'un désastre
Aérien qui me ramènerait Melody
Mineure détournée de l'attraction des astres

***

Lui – **Tu t'appelles comment**
Elle – **Melody**
Lui – **Melody comment**
Elle – **Melody Nelson**

Paroles et musique de Serge Gainsbourg
© Editions et Productions Sidonie/Warner Chappell Music France/
Melody Nelson Publishing

EVER THE PROVOCATEUR

In between concept albums, Serge puts out *Vu de l'extérieur,* but not before sustaining a heart attack on May 15th, 1973. He spends a week recovering at the American Hospital in Neuilly, just outside of Paris. Serge continued to smoke, albeit clandestinely, during his stay there. Six months later, "Serge gives the magazine *Spectacle* an interview in the form of a confession, which is broadcast on television on November 3rd, 1973:

'I had some friends. Now I'll have fewer. I'm becoming a little more difficult. I was already a misogynist, and now I'm a misanthrope. You see, there's not much that remains, but I still have the essentials, like my children, my wife, and my work. That continues. With a more lucid mind and hands that no longer tremble – or at least very rarely. Alcohol had a very harmful effect on me. I was so completely saturated that I'd go all night long without any inspiration. I was moving really fast and I saw all sorts of landscapes pass me by, but I'd hit a wall. Now I know I have a minor heart condition, and I hope it won't get too serious. I hope I'll survive.'"[109]

Vu de l'extérieur is seductively carnal, unabashedly scatological, and sells a mere 20,000 copies. It is a commercial failure. "Gainsbourg may not be selling to the masses, but he's always on the radio and on television. Each time he makes an appearance, he says something nobody else would dare say, champions a position nobody else would dare champion. He smokes, he's unshaven, he curses, he's cynical, he lip-synchs, and each time, his songs – without fail – contain something that will shock daddy or grandma. The little eight- to twelve-year-old brats who see Gainsbourg in the seventies may not be old enough to buy his records, yet for some of them, something electric is happening. They see something in this 45-year-old punk. Once he finds the right musical vehicle, things will take off."[110]

109 Gainsbourg, Verlant, **2000**, Albin Michel. Translation by Paul Knobloch.
110 Gainsbourg, Verlant, **2000**, Albin Michel. Translation by Paul Knobloch.

LA DÉCADANSE [1971]

This song was intended to be a "vertical sequel" to 1967's *Je t'aime moi non plus*. It openly evokes sodomy, with Gainsbourg explaining in 1972 that "the 'décadanse'[111] is nothing but an inverted slow dance. It's true that the woman turns her back to her partner... I don't see what's so shocking about that!"*

HIM – *Turn around*
HER – *No...* HIM – *Come close*
HER – *No, not like that...* HIM – And dance
The décadanse
Yes, that's good
Swing your hips
Slowly in front of mine

HER – Stay there
Behind me
Back and forth
The décadanse
Have your hands
Stroke my breasts
And the heart that belongs to you

HIM – *My love*
My life-long love
Be patient
The décadanse
Under the spell of my touch
Will take you
To faraway lands

HER – Troubled waters
Suddenly muddle
My senses
The décadanse
Will be the end of me
Ah! You are killing me
My love, tell me, do you love me

HIM – *I loved you*
Already but[112]

---

111 "Décadanse" ("danse" = "dance") is a neologism pronounced exactly the same way as "décadence", which means "decline" or "decay".

112 The French couplet is: "Je t'aimais / Déjà mais". "Déjà" means "already", and "mais" means "but". However, if one fuses the two words of the second verse, the word "jamais" appears, which means "never". The effect is similar to the one created by the famous "je t'aime moi non plus" verse.**

LA DÉCADANSE

LUI – *Tourne-toi*
ELLE – *Non...* LUI – *Contre moi*
ELLE – *Non, pas comme ça...* LUI – Et danse
La décadanse
Oui, c'est bien
Bouge tes reins
Lentement devant les miens

ELLE – Reste là
Derrière moi
Balance
La décadanse
Que tes mains
Frôlent mes seins
Et mon cœur qui est le tien

LUI – *Mon amour*
De toujours
Patience
La décadanse
Sous mes doigts
T'emmènera
Vers de lointains au-delà

ELLE – Des eaux troubles
Soudain troublent
Mes sens
La décadanse
M'a perdue
Ah ! tu me tues
Mon amour, dis, m'aimes-tu

LUI – *Je t'aimais*
Déjà mais

Nuance
The décadanse
More so even
Than death
Fuses our souls and bodies

HER – May the gods forgive
Us our
Trespasses
The décadanse
Has soothed
Our frozen bodies
And our lost souls

HIM – *May the gods forgive*
Us our
Trespasses
The décadanse
Has soothed
Our jaded bodies
And our lost souls

Nuance
La décadanse
Plus encore
Que notre mort
Lie nos âmes et nos corps

ELLE – Dieux pardo-
Nnez nos
Offenses
La décadanse
A bercé
Nos corps glacés
Et nos âmes égarées

LUI – *Dieux pardo-*
Nnez nos
Offenses
La décadanse
A bercé
Nos corps blasés
Et nos âmes égarées

Paroles et musique Serge Gainsbourg
© Warner Chappell Music France/Melody Nelson Publishing

SEX SHOP [1972]

This song is part of the soundtrack for Claude Berri's 1972 film *Sex Shop*, in which a bankrupt bookseller decides to begin dealing in pornography.*

The lyrics are crude but the emotion is palpable; Gainsbourg's delivery does not gloss over the pain of having been cheated on.

Hey, you little slut, tell me
What it was like to be in his arms
Was it better than being with me

Yeah, you little vixen, tell me everything
How many times, how many trysts
You didn't actually go all the way[113]

No, you little slut, you're lying to me
He didn't do to you
All that you say he did

But, you little cunt,[114] it matters not
Describe again to me his hands
On your stomach and on your breasts

You didn't actually, you didn't do
That to me, it's not true
Tell me it's not true

Hey, you little slut, tell me
What it was like to be in his arms
Was it better than being with me

But, you little bitch, if you've told me the truth
Never will I forgive you
I swear to you, never

Liar
Liar

---

113 This is not a declarative statement; there is a tacit "did you?" at the end of the sentence. The French "quand même pas" denotes incredulity.

114 Gainsbourg uses the word "conne", which is usually translated as meaning "asshole" (see 1968's *Requiem pour un con*). However, your translator felt it necessary to keep the insults very feminine, just as Gainsbourg did. Also, the origins of the word "conne" can be traced back to the latin "cunnus", meaning "furrow" and by association, "vagina". As a result, the choice of the word "cunt" has a modicum of etymological standing.

SEX SHOP

Dis, petite salope, raconte-moi
Comment c'était entre ses bras
Était-ce mieux qu'avec moi

Ouais, petite vicieuse, dis-moi tout
Combien de fois, combien de coups
Quand même pas jusqu'au bout

Non, petite salope, tu me mens
Il ne t'en a pas fait autant
Que tu ne le prétends

Mais, petite conne, ça ne fait rien
Invente-moi encore ses mains
Sur ton ventre et tes seins

Quand même, tu m'as pas fait
Ça, c'est pas vrai
Dis-moi qu'c'est pas vrai

Dis, petite salope, redis-moi
Comment c'était entre ses bras
Était-ce mieux qu'avec moi

Mais, petite garce, si tu m'as dit vrai
Je ne te pardonnerai
Je te jure, jamais

Menteuse
Menteuse

Paroles Serge Gainsbourg
Musique Serge Gainsbourg & Jean-Claude Vannier
© Bagatelle/Hortensia

JE SUIS VENU TE DIRE QUE JE M'EN VAIS – I'VE COME TO TELL YOU THAT I'M LEAVING [1973]

This is the first song off the album *Vu de l'extérieur*, which was nearly complete when Gainsbourg had a heart attack on May 15th, 1973.

Many mistakenly believe this to be a breakup song directed at Jane Birkin. In reality, the two would stay together until 1980.

I've come to tell you that I'm leaving
And your tears are powerless to stop me
In Verlaine's[115] fine words, "On an ill wind"
I've come to tell you that I'm leaving

You remember the old days and you cry
You wheeze, you turn pale, now that the bell has tolled
Goodbye for good
Yep, I'm sorry to have to
Tell you that I'm leaving
Yep I loved you, yes but

I've come to tell you that I'm leaving
And your sobbing is powerless to stop me
In Verlaine's fine words, "On an ill wind"
I've come to tell you that I'm leaving

You remember the happy days and you cry
You sob, you wail, now that the bell has tolled
Goodbye for good
Yep, I'm sorry to have to
Tell you that I'm leaving
Because you've done me wrong for too long

I've come to tell you that I'm leaving
And your tears are powerless to stop me

---

115 Paul Verlaine (1844-1896) was a famous French poet. This song's lyrics draw heavily from his poem *Chanson d'automne*, one of the most admired works in French literary history. An attempt at a translation is provided below.

Chanson d'automne – Autumn Song (from *Poèmes Saturniens*, **1867**)
The long sobs/Of the autumn/Violins/Pierce my heart/With their monotonous/Languor/Wheezing/ And pale, as/The bell tolls,/I remember/The old days/And I weep/And I'm leaving/On an ill wind/ That sends me/Hither, thither,/Not unlike/A dead leaf

As a historical aside, the BBC had indicated to the French Résistance in 1944 that the first stanza of this poem would be broadcast to signal the beginning of D-Day operations. The first three lines were broadcast on June 1st, and the next three were heard on June 5th.

For more on Verlaine, see *La Noyée* [1971].

JE SUIS VENU TE DIRE QUE JE M'EN VAIS

Je suis venu te dire que je m'en vais
Et tes larmes n'y pourront rien changer
Comme dit si bien Verlaine, "Au vent mauvais"
Je suis venu te dire que je m'en vais

Tu t'souviens des jours anciens et tu pleures
Tu suffoques, tu blêmis, à présent qu'a sonné l'heure
Des adieux à jamais
Oui, je suis au regret
De te dire que je m'en vais
Oui je t'aimais, oui mais

Je suis venu te dire que je m'en vais
Tes sanglots longs n'y pourront rien changer
Comme dit si bien Verlaine, "Au vent mauvais"
Je suis venu te dire que je m'en vais

Tu t'souviens des jours heureux et tu pleures
Tu sanglotes, tu gémis, à présent qu'a sonné l'heure
Des adieux à jamais
Oui, je suis au regret
De te dire que je m'en vais
Car tu m'en as trop fait

Je suis venu te dire que je m'en vais
Et tes larmes n'y pourront rien changer

In Verlaine's fine words, "On an ill wind"
I've come to tell you that I'm leaving

You remember the old days and you cry
You suffocate, you turn pale, now that the bell has tolled
Goodbye for good
Yep, I'm sorry to have to
Tell you that I'm leaving
Yep I loved you, yes but

I've come to tell you that I'm leaving
And your tears are powerless to stop me
In Verlaine's fine words, "On an ill wind"
I've come to tell you that I'm leaving

You remember the happy days and you cry
You sob, you wail, now that the bell has tolled
Goodbye for good
Yep, I'm sorry to have to
Tell you that I'm leaving
Because you've done me wrong for too long

Comme dit si bien Verlaine, "Au vent mauvais"
Je suis venu te dire que je m'en vais

Tu t'souviens des jours anciens et tu pleures
Tu suffoques, tu blêmis, à présent qu'a sonné l'heure
Des adieux à jamais
Oui, je suis au regret
De te dire que je m'en vais
Oui je t'aimais, oui mais

Je suis venu te dire que je m'en vais
Tes sanglots longs n'y pourront rien changer
Comme dit si bien Verlaine, "Au vent mauvais"
Je suis venu te dire que je m'en vais

Tu t'souviens des jours heureux et tu pleures
Tu sanglotes, tu gémis, à présent qu'a sonné l'heure
Des adieux à jamais
Oui, je suis au regret
De te dire que je m'en vais
Car tu m'en as trop fait

Paroles et musique Serge Gainsbourg
© 1974 by Melody Nelson Publishing

VU DE L'EXTÉRIEUR — ON THE OUTSIDE [1973]

A song about breasts, butts and the inability to found a lasting relationship on the strength of these two attributes alone. Although the lyrics certainly lack substance, the song – taken as a whole – is quite beautiful.

You're pretty, on the outside
Alas, I'm familiar with all that goes on inside
It ain't pretty, it's actually quite nasty
So don't be surprised if today I tell you to go to hell

Go to hell
And make sure to take with you
Your knockers
So soft, so silky
And your posterior

It's pretty, on the outside
Woe to me for having penetrated inside
It was a good time, obviously
But you know as well as I do that such moments are finite

Go to hell
And make sure to take with you
Your tits
So pretty, so warm
And your big round ass

It's pretty, on the outside
God, whatever possessed me to go poking around inside
It was a good time, obviously
But you know as well as I do that such moments are finite

Go to hell
And make sure to take with you
Your two cans
Your big jugs
And your cute little ass

It's pretty, on the outside
I should have known, I shouldn't have risked going inside
It was a good time, obviously
But you know as well as I do that such moments are finite

Go to hell
And make sure to take with you
Seriously, don't forget
Your milk bags

VU DE L'EXTÉRIEUR

Tu es belle, vue de l'extérieur
Hélas ! je connais tout c'qui se passe à l'intérieur
C'est pas beau, même assez dégoûtant
Alors ne t'étonne pas si aujourd'hui je te dis "Va-t'en"

Va t'faire voir
Va faire voir ailleurs
Tes roudoudous
Tout mous, tout doux
Et ton postérieur

Il est beau, vu de l'extérieur
Malheur à moi qui ai pénétré à l'intérieur
C'était bon, ça évidemment
Mais tu sais comme moi que ces choses-là n'ont qu'un temps

Va t'faire voir
Va faire voir ailleurs
Tes roploplos
Tout beaux, tout chauds
Et ton gros pétard

Il est beau, vu de l'extérieur
Qu'est-ce qui m'a pris, grands dieux, d'm'aventurer à l'intérieur
C'était bon, ça évidemment
Mais tu sais comme moi que ces choses-là n'ont qu'un temps

Va faire voir
Va faire voir ailleurs
Tes deux doudounes
Tes gros balloons
Et ton p'tit valseur

Il est beau, vu de l'extérieur
J'aurais dû me méfier, pas m'risquer à l'intérieur
C'était bon, ça évidemment
Mais tu sais comme moi que ces choses-là n'ont qu'un temps

Va t'faire voir
Va faire voir ailleurs
Et sans délai
Tes boîtes à lait

And your derrière

It's pretty, on the outside
Woe to me for having risked going inside
It was a good time, obviously
But you know as well as I do that such moments are finite

Go to hell
And make sure to take with you
Your pretty pillows
Soft as marshmallows
And your caboose

It's pretty, on the outside
But you're as familiar as I am with what goes on inside
It ain't pretty, it's actually quite nasty
So don't be surprised if today I tell you to go to hell

Go to hell
And make sure to take with you

Et ton popotin

Il est beau, vu de l'extérieur
Pauvre de moi qui m'suis risqué à l'intérieur
C'était bon, ça évidemment
Mais tu sais comme moi que ces choses-là n'ont qu'un temps

Va t'faire voir
Va faire voir ailleurs
Tes beaux lolos
En marshmallow
Et ton p'tit panier

Il est beau, vu de l'extérieur
Mais tu sais comme moi tout ce qui s'passe à l'intérieur
C'est pas beau, même assez dégoûtant
Alors ne t'étonne pas si aujourd'hui je te dis "Va-t'en"

Va t'faire voir
Va t'faire voir ailleurs

Paroles et musique Serge Gainsbourg
© 1974 by Melody Nelson Publishing

COMME UN BOOMERANG — LIKE A BOOMERANG [1975]

This track was first recorded in 1975 by French singer Dani, and was subsequently submitted to the selection committee for that year's Eurovision contest. However, a lighter-themed song by Nicole Rieu (*Et bonjour à toi l'artiste*) was chosen instead. *Comme un boomerang* then proceeded to fall into relative anonymity.*

Twenty-five years later, in 2001, a singer named Étienne Daho happened upon the track and re-recorded it as a duet with Dani. The single went on to win Best Song of the Year at the *Victoires de la Musique** (French equivalent of the Grammy Awards or Brit Awards), thus completing its boomerang-like comeback.

I feel BOOMS! and BANGS!
Trouble my wounded heart
Love, like a boomerang
Comes back to me from days spent
Crying the crazy tears
Of a body I had given to you

I have on the tip of my tongue
Your nearly-forgotten name
Warped like a boomerang
My soul refused it entry
To my memory, because the partying
And your love both drained me

I feel BOOMS! and BANGS!
Trouble my wounded heart
Love, like a boomerang
Comes back to me from days spent
Loving each other like crazy
Fit to be tied fools

Know that this weary heart
Could one day stop beating
If like a boomerang
You don't come back to get me
Little by little, I'm becoming unglued
A victim of your cruelty

I feel BOOMS! and BANGS!
Trouble my wounded heart
Love, like a boomerang
Comes back to me from days spent
Loving you like crazy
I'd go to hell and back for you

You belong to the same gang

COMME UN BOOMERANG

Je sens des BOUM ! et des BANG !
Agiter mon cœur blessé
L'amour comme un boomerang
Me revient des jours passés
À pleurer les larmes dingues
D'un corps que je t'avais donné

J'ai sur le bout de la langue
Ton prénom presque effacé
Tordu comme un boomerang
Mon esprit l'a rejeté
De ma mémoire, car la bringue
Et ton amour m'ont épuisée

Je sens des BOUM ! et des BANG !
Agiter mon cœur blessé
L'amour comme un boomerang
Me revient des jours passés
À s'aimer comme des dingues
Comme deux fous à lier

Sache que ce cœur exsangue
Pourrait un jour s'arrêter
Si comme un boomerang
Tu n'reviens pas me chercher
Peu à peu, je me déglingue
Victime de ta cruauté

Je sens des BOUM ! et des BANG !
Agiter mon cœur blessé
L'amour comme un boomerang
Me revient des jours passés
À t'aimer comme une dingue
Prête pour toi à me damner

Toi qui fais partie du gang

As my seducers past
Take notice of this boomerang
It could make you pay
For all the twisted torture
You had me endure

I feel BOOMS! and BANGS!
Trouble my wounded heart
Love, like a boomerang
Comes back to me from the old days
It's a crazy story
A silly old story

My sanity wavers and lists
It's about ready to sink
Under the blows of the boomerang
And of the constant flashbacks
And if one day I shoot myself
I'll owe the deed to you

I feel BOOMS! and BANGS!
Trouble my wounded heart
Love, like a boomerang
Comes back to me from days spent
Crying the crazy tears
Of a body I had given you

De mes séducteurs passés
Prends garde à ce boomerang
Il pourrait te faire payer
Toutes ces tortures de cing-
Lé que tu m'as fait endurer

Je sens des BOUM ! et des BANG !
Agiter mon cœur blessé
L'amour, comme un boomerang
Me revient des jours passés
C'est une histoire de dingue
Une histoire bête à pleurer

Ma raison vacille et tangue
Elle est prête à chavirer
Sous les coups de boomerang
Des flash-backs enchaînés
Et si un jour je me flingue
C'est à toi que je le devrai

Je sens des BOUM ! et des BANG !
Agiter mon cœur blessé
L'amour comme un boomerang
Me revient des jours passés
À pleurer les larmes dingues
D'un corps que je t'avais donné

Paroles et musique Serge Gainsbourg
© Melody Nelson Publishing

ROCK AROUND THE BUNKER

Slighted by critics upon its release, this second concept album served primarily to exorcise Serge's childhood demons, thereby constituting a self-admittedly necessary catharsis for the singer.

Gainsbourg's parents, Joseph and Olia Ginsburg, were Russian Jews who fled the Bolshevik revolution and moved to the French capital in 1919, only to be uprooted again when the Nazis invaded France. Gainsbourg's father, a cabaret pianist, was forced to leave the occupied zone in 1942 to find work, leaving his family behind. As the hunt for Jews intensified in Paris, the rest of the family joined him in the Limousin region in 1944. All three children (Serge had two sisters, Jacqueline and Liliane) were hidden away as boarders in religious institutions. Serge was enrolled in a Jesuit school under the alias Lucien Guimbard (Lucien was Serge's birth name and Guimbard replaced the telltale Jewish last name). One evening, Serge was sent out alone to the surrounding forest; the school's directors had learned that the Gestapo was to conduct a raid that night to hunt for Jewish hide-aways enrolled at the institution.

Suffice it to say that Serge was scarred by these experiences, although he often chose to deal with the past humorously. For example, the yellow star he was forced to wear is compared to a sheriff's badge in *Yellow Star,* a track off *Rock Around the Bunker.* Serge's incisive and unapologetic sense of humor is on full display throughout the album.

NAZI ROCK [1975]

This track tells the story of the Night of the Long Knives: between June 30th and July 2nd, 1934, Hitler purged men of influence perceived as hostile to his government. Many of those killed were members of the Sturmabteilung (the SA), while the massacre was perpetrated by the Schutzstaffel (the SS) and the Gestapo. The SA was a paramilitary organization whose leader, Ernst Röhm, was viewed as a major threat by Hitler. Röhm and other SA leaders were homosexual, a fact that Hitler's minister of propaganda, Joseph Goebbels, made public following the Night of the Long Knives. Gainsbourg seems to riff on this detail in his song, joyously turning all Nazis into affected transvestites.

HIM – *The night of the long knives is upon us*

Put your black stockings on guys
Make sure your suspender slings fit properly
Your garter belts and corsets too
Come on, it's about to get hairy

We're going to dance the
CHORISTS – Nazi Rock, Nazi
Nazi, Nazi Rock, Nazi
HIM – Yeah, we're going to dance the
CHORISTS – Nazi Rock, Nazi
Nazi, Nazi Rock, Nazi

HIM – Put your lipstick on guys
Make your mouths really pop
Choose delicate shades of red
Or black or blue if that's what you fancy

Chorus

HIM – Put hairspray and gel in
Your blond locks guys
Apply foundation and blush liberally
Come now before it's too late

Chorus

HIM – We're going to dance the
CHORISTS – Nazi Rock, Nazi
Nazi, Nazi Rock, Nazi
HIM – We're going to dance the
CHORISTS – Nazi Rock, Nazi
Nazi, Nazi Rock, Nazi
HIM – Yeah, we're going to dance the
CHORISTS – Nazi Rock, Nazi
Nazi, Nazi Rock, Nazi

NAZI ROCK

Lui – *Voici venir la nuit des longs couteaux*

Enfilez vos bas noirs les gars
Ajustez bien vos accroche-bas
Vos porte-jarretelles et vos corsets
Allez venez, ça va s'corser

On va danser le
Chœurs – Nazi Rock, Nazi
Nazi, Nazi Rock, Nazi
Lui – Ouais, on va danser le
Chœurs – Nazi Rock, Nazi
Nazi, Nazi Rock, Nazi

Lui – Maquillez vos lèvres les gars
Avec des rouges délicats
Faites-vous des bouches sanglantes
Ou noires ou bleues si ça vous tente

Refrain

Lui – Sur vos boucles blondes les gars
Mettez fixatifs et corps gras
N'épargnez ni onguents ni fards
Venez avant qu'il soit trop tard

Refrain

Lui – On va danser le
Chœurs – Nazi Rock, Nazi
Nazi, Nazi Rock, Nazi
Lui – On va danser le
Chœurs – Nazi Rock, Nazi
Nazi, Nazi Rock, Nazi
Lui – Ouais, on va danser le
Chœurs – Nazi Rock, Nazi
Nazi, Nazi Rock, Nazi

HIM – We're going to dance the
CHORISTS – Nazi Rock, Nazi
Nazi, Nazi Rock, Nazi
HIM – We're going to dance the
CHORISTS – Nazi Rock, Nazi
Nazi, Nazi Rock, Nazi
HIM – We're going to dance the
CHORISTS – Nazi Rock, Nazi
Nazi, Nazi Rock, Nazi
HIM – Yeah, we're going to dance the
CHORISTS – Nazi Rock, Nazi
Nazi, Nazi Rock, Nazi
HIM – We're going to dance the
CHORISTS – Nazi Rock, Nazi
Nazi, Nazi Rock, Nazi
HIM – We're going to dance the
CHORISTS – Nazi Rock, Nazi
Nazi, Nazi Rock, Nazi
HIM – We're going to dance the
CHORISTS – Nazi Rock, Nazi
Nazi, Nazi Rock, Nazi
HIM – Yeah, we're going to dance the
CHORISTS – Nazi Rock, Nazi
Nazi, Nazi Rock, Nazi
HIM – We're going to dance the
CHORISTS – Nazi Rock, Nazi
Nazi, Nazi Rock, Nazi
HIM – We're going to dance the
CHORISTS – Nazi Rock, Nazi
Nazi, Nazi Rock, Nazi

Lui – On va danser le
Chœurs – Nazi Rock, Nazi
Nazi, Nazi Rock, Nazi
Lui – On va danser le
Chœurs – Nazi Rock, Nazi
Nazi, Nazi Rock, Nazi
Lui – On va danser le
Chœurs – Nazi Rock, Nazi
Nazi, Nazi Rock, Nazi
Lui – Ouais, on va danser le
Chœurs – Nazi Rock, Nazi
Nazi, Nazi Rock, Nazi
Lui – On va danser le
Chœurs – Nazi Rock, Nazi
Nazi, Nazi Rock, Nazi
Lui – On va danser le
Chœurs – Nazi Rock, Nazi
Nazi, Nazi Rock, Nazi
Lui – On va danser le
Chœurs – Nazi Rock, Nazi
Nazi, Nazi Rock, Nazi
Lui – Ouais, on va danser le
Chœurs – Nazi Rock, Nazi
Nazi, Nazi Rock, Nazi
Lui – On va danser le
Chœurs – Nazi Rock, Nazi
Nazi, Nazi Rock, Nazi
Lui – On va danser le
Chœurs – Nazi Rock, Nazi
Nazi, Nazi Rock, Nazi

Paroles et musique Serge Gainsbourg
© 1975 by Melody Nelson Publishing

SS IN URUGUAY [1975]

After World War II, a large number of Nazis fled to South America through well-orga-
nized escape routes (appropriately dubbed "ratlines"). Argentina was a favorite destination of theirs, but other countries such as Paraguay, Brazil, Chile, Bolivia and Uruguay
were also quite welcoming.

CHORISTS – SS in Uruguay
HIM – Sporting a straw hat
I sip papaya juice
Through a straw

CHORISTS – SS in Uruguay
HIM – Under the beating sun
Memories haunt me
Ay ay ay

Morons speak
Of extradition
But for me settling the tab
Is out of the question[116]

CHORISTS – SS in Uruguay
HIM – I was just a figurehead
But I fear retribution
Wherever I go

CHORISTS – SS in Uruguay
HIM – Sporting a straw hat
I sip papaya juice
Through a straw

CHORISTS – SS in Uruguay
HIM – I've kept as battle souvenirs
Enamel swastikas
And medals

And those morons still speak
Of extradition
But for me settling the tab
Is out of the question

---

116 In the chorus, Gainsbourg sings the last word of every verse with a latin accent.

SS IN URUGUAY

CHŒURS – SS in Uruguay
LUI – Sous un chapeau de paille
J'siffle un jus de papaye
Avec paille

CHŒURS – SS in Uruguay
LUI – Sous le soleil duraille
Les souvenirs m'assaillent
Aïe, aïe, aïe

Il y a des couillonnes
Qui parlent d'extraditionne
Mais pour moi pas questionne
De payer l'additionne

CHŒURS – SS in Uruguay
LUI – J'n'étais qu'un homme de paille
Mais j'crains des représailles
Où que j'aille

CHŒURS – SS in Uruguay
LUI – Sous un chapeau de paille
J'siffle un jus de papaye
Avec paille

CHŒURS – SS in Uruguay
LUI – J'ai gardé d'mes batailles
Croix gammée et médailles
En émail

Et toujours ces couillonnes
Qui parlent d'extraditionne
Mais pour moi pas questionne
De payer l'additionne

CHORISTS – SS in Uruguay
HIM – Here, I'm surrounded by henchmen
Who wait on me hand, Heil!
And foot

CHŒURS – SS in Uruguay
LUI – J'ai ici d'la canaille
Qui m'obéit au doigt, hei-
L ! et à l'œil

Paroles et musique Serge Gainsbourg
© 1975 by Melody Nelson Publishing

THIRD AND FINAL CONCEPT ALBUM: L'HOMME À TÊTE DE CHOU

After Melody Nelson comes Marilou, the heroine of Gainsbourg's magnificent concept album, *L'Homme à tête de chou (The Cabbage-Head Man)*. Inspired by a Claude Lalanne statue he had purchased – whose likeness graces the album cover – Gainsbourg tells the story of a struggling journalist taken with a young shampoo-girl who ends up cheating on him with rock musicians. Under the strain of Marilou's caustic abuse, our cuckold's ears turn into cabbage leaves and he becomes a chain-smoking alcoholic. Finally, in a jealous rage, the journalist beats Marilou to death with a fire extinguisher before ultimately being committed to a mental institution.

The album was a commercial failure upon release, selling only 25,000 copies.[117] It would take until the release of the smash hit *Aux armes et cætera* in 1979 for *L'Homme à tête de chou* to receive proper recognition.

L'homme à tête de chou sees Gainsbourg trying his hand at reggae for the first time, and he does so with aplomb. *Marilou Reggae* is a stellar track that he would revisit on the very same *Aux armes et cætera*.

---

117 Gainsbourg, Verlant, **2000**, Albin Michel.

Serge at home with Bambou on October 14ᵗʰ, 1981. L'homme à tête de chou
*by Claude Lalanne is off to Serge's left. For more on Bambou,
see introductory notes to* La nostalgie camarade *[1981].*

Photo by Jean-Claude Deutsch

L'HOMME À TÊTE DE CHOU — THE CABBAGE-HEAD MAN [1976]

The first track off the album is a first-person plot summary seemingly told from the psychiatric ward where our jilted journalist has taken up residence. From this point on, the rest of the album's songs take on the feel of flashbacks.

I'm the cabbage-head man
Half-vegetable, half-human
For Marilou's pretty eyes
I went to pawn off
My Remington[118] and my station wagon
I'd had it, I was at the end
Of my rope, I was penniless
From the day I got with
Her, I lost almost everything
My job at the rag[119]
That brought the dough in
I was done, fucked, check
Mate in Marilou's eyes
She treated me like a callow greenhorn
And drove me half-mad
Ah! No, if you only knew, man
She needed to go to the discos
And eat out at the Kangaroo
Club, so I wrote
Bad checks, I was crazy, crazy
In the end, I made her head swell
To the size of a watermelon
But hold on a sec, I'm not just going to
Tell all like this, so quickly
What, me, still love her? Nuts
Who and where am I, a cabbage here, or
In the white surf, a piece of seaweed
On the beach in Malibu

---

118 The classic typewriter manufacturer had already been referenced in Gainsbourg's *Elaeudanla Téïtéïa* [1963]. In this song, the title and chorus consist of a spelling of the first name "Lætitia"; the narrator mentions that he has committed the name to posterity using a portable Remington typewriter.

119 Gainsbourg uses the slang term "feuille de chou", which in context means "a substandard newspaper" or, more fittingly, "a rag". In French, the use of the expression artfully echoes the song's title.

L'HOMME À TÊTE DE CHOU

Je suis l'homme à tête de chou
Moitié légume, moitié mec
Pour les beaux yeux de Marilou
Je suis allé porter au clou
Ma Remington et puis mon break
J'étais à fond de cale, à bout
De nerfs, j'avais plus un kopeck
Du jour où j'me mis avec
Elle, je perdis à peu près tout
Mon job à la feuille de chou
À scandales qui m'donnait le bifteck
J'étais fini, foutu, échec
Et mat aux yeux de Marilou
Qui m'traitait comme un blanc-bec
Et m'rendait moitié coucou
Ah ! non, tu peux pas savoir, mec
Il lui fallait les discothèques
Et bouffer au Kangourou
Club, alors j'signais des chèques
Sans provision, j'étais fou, fou
À la fin, j'y fis l'caillou
Comme un melon, une pastèque
Mais moment, j'vais pas tout
Déballer comme ça aussi sec
Quoi, moi, l'aimer encore ? Des clous
Qui et où suis-je, chou ici, ou
Dans la blanche écume, varech
Sur la plage de Malibu

Paroles et musique de Serge Gainsbourg
© 1977 by Melody Nelson Publishing

CHEZ MAX COIFFEUR POUR HOMMES — AT MAX'S BARBERSHOP [1976]

The story of the first encounter between the narrator and Marilou.

At Max's barbershop
Where I went one day on
A whim to have a shave
And a trim, I run into this vixen
This shampoo-girl
Who immediately blinds me with her pagan beauty
And her soapy hands

She leans over, and there go her tits
Like two rosewater Turkish delights
Bouncing on the nape of my neck, BOOM BOOM

She reminds me of the Caliph's daughter
On the thousand-and-second night
And I feel the tip of a pocketknife
Pierce my heart, I tell her

"Girl, I'm taking you out tonight, OK"
She first lets out a little laugh like a hic-
Cup, then, over the din
Of the blow-dryer
In my hair
The little bitch murmurs
"Take me"

CHEZ MAX COIFFEUR POUR HOMMES

Chez Max, coiffeur pour hommes
Où un jour j'entrais comme
Par hasard me faire raser la couenne
Et rafraîchir les douilles, je tombe sur cette chienne
Shampooineuse
Qui aussitôt m'aveugle par sa beauté païenne
Et ses mains savonneuses

Elle se penche, et voilà ses doudounes
Comme deux rahat-loukoums
À la rose qui rebondissent sur ma nuque, BOUM BOUM !

Je pense à la fille du Calife
De la mille et deuxième nuit
Et sens la pointe d'un canif
Me percer le cœur, je lui dis

"Petite, j'te sors ce soir, OK"
Elle a d'abord un petit rire comme un hoqu-
Et, puis, sous le siroc-
Co du séchoir
Dans mes cheveux
La petite garce laisse choir
"Je veux"

Paroles et musique Serge Gainsbourg
© 1977 by Melody Nelson Publishing

FLASH FORWARD [1976]

Marilou's cheating ways are exposed.

One night, unannounced, BAM!
I knock on my door, KNOCK KNOCK!
No answer, I push it open
And, I listen to the bed frame groan
And the box spring creak
I move forward in the black-
Out, and my Kodak
Impresses visions of a brothel upon
The sensitive plates of my brain
I feel my heartbeat
Swiftly shift to mach
Two, TIC-TAC! TIC-TAC! TIC-TAC! TIC-TAC!
As though it had been electro-shocked
She was between two baboons
Of the Woodstock festival variety
And resembled a two-jacked
Rock guitar
One guy at her birth-hole, the other at her asshole, CRACK![120]
Hey! Doc
Who, me, paranoid
Why don't you go ask the old geezer
The night-watchman at the Roxy
Hotel if I'm crazy
It's there, for posterity, on the note-
Pad of my memory, in black
And white, and whatever
I do, it'll come back to me in flashbacks
Damn it! Until it kills me

---

120 As Gainsbourg aged, his use of talk-over (*i.e.* spoken word) increased. By way of explanation, Gainsbourg evoked this particular verse: "*I do so-called 'talk-over' because [...] you can't sing 'One guy at her birth-hole, the other at her asshole', it's not possible, you have to say it. Very nice alexandrine by the way.*"

FLASH FORWARD

Un soir qu'à l'improviste, CHTAC !
Je frappe à ma porte, TOC TOC !
Sans réponse, je pousse le loqu-
Et, j'écoute gémir le hamac
Grincer les ressorts du paddock
J'avance dans le black-
Out, et mon Kodak
Impressionne sur les plaques
Sensibles de mon cerveau une vision de claque
Je sens mon rythme cardiaque
Qui passe brusquement à mach
Deux, TIC-TAC ! TIC-TAC ! TIC-TAC ! TIC-TAC !
Comme sous un électrochoc
Elle était entre deux macaques
Du genre festival à Woodstock
Et semblait une guitare rock
À deux jacks
L'un à son trou d'obus, l'autre à son trou de balle, CRAC !
Eh ! doc
Qui, moi, paranoïaque
Demandez donc un peu au vioque
Qui est portier de nuit au Rox-
Y Hôtel si j'débloque
C'est là, à jamais, sur le bloc-
Notes de ma mémoire, black
Sur white, et quoi qu'
Je fasse, ça m'reviendra en flash-back
Bordel ! jusqu'à c'que j'en claque

Paroles et musique Serge Gainsbourg
© 1977 Melody Nelson Publishing

MA LOU MARILOU — MY LOU MARILOU [1976]

In this number, a jaunty melody masks impossibly dark lyrics. This is similar to the formula used for 1966's *Baby Pop*, although here the theme is explicitly sexual.

So begins our jilted journalist's descent into madness, with a melody borrowing heavily from a theme found in the first movement of Beethoven's Sonata no. 23 *Appassionata*.

> CHORISTS – Oh! my Lou, oh! my Lou
> HIM – Oh! Marilou
> Little wench
> Shampoo-girl
> Of my dreams
>
> **CHORISTS – Oh! my Lou, oh! my Lou**
> **HIM – Oh! Marilou**
> **If you flinch, I'll wring your neck**
>
> CHORISTS – Oh! my Lou, oh! my Lou
> HIM – Oh! Marilou
> You better
> Behave
> Life is short
>
> **CHORISTS – Oh! my Lou, oh! my Lou**
> **HIM – Oh! Marilou**
> **One wrong move, I'll lock you up**
>
> CHORISTS – Oh! my Lou, oh! my Lou
> HIM – Oh! Marilou
> My monogamous
> Soul is yours
> As is my seed[121]
>
> **CHORISTS – Oh! my Lou, oh! my Lou**
> **HIM – Oh! Marilou**
> **Bottom line, you're going to get it**
>
> CHORISTS – Oh! my Lou, oh! my Lou
> HIM – Oh! Marilou
> I love your two

---

121 Literally translated, this would read "as is my sap".

MA LOU MARILOU

CHŒURS – Oh ! ma Lou, oh ! ma Lou
LUI – Oh ! Marilou
Petite gueuse
Shampooineuse
De mes rêves

CHŒURS – Oh ! ma Lou, oh ! ma Lou
LUI – Oh ! Marilou
Si tu bronches, je te tords le cou

CHŒURS – Oh ! ma Lou, oh ! ma Lou
LUI – Oh ! Marilou
Tiens-toi à
Carreau la
Vie est brève

CHŒURS – Oh ! ma Lou, oh ! ma Lou
LUI – Oh ! Marilou
Un faux-pas, et t'voilà au trou

CHŒURS – Oh ! ma Lou, oh ! ma Lou
LUI – Oh ! Maribou
Tu as mon âme
Monogame
Et ma sève

CHŒURS – Oh ! ma Lou, oh ! ma Lou
LUI – Oh ! Marilou
C'est pour toi, et un point c'est tout

CHŒURS – Oh ! ma Lou, oh ! ma Lou
LUI – Oh ! Marilou
J'aime tes deux

Breasts, your eyes,
And your charm[122]

CHORISTS – Oh! my Lou, oh! my Lou
HIM – Oh! Marilou
Be careful or I'll knock your lights out[123]

---

122 The word "fève" is used in the original lyrics, which means either "bean" or "charm placed in a king cake". Your translator chose to play off the second definition; in either case, it is clear that this is a thinly veiled reference to Marilou's clitoris. Note: a "king cake" is a marzipan-rich confection traditionally baked to celebrate Epiphany.

123 In French, the expression "rentrer dans le chou" is used, which means "to attack someone violently". Another clever reference to the album's title, and further proof of Gainsbourg's absolute mastery of the French language.

Seins, tes yeux
Et ta fève

CHŒURS – Oh ! ma Lou, oh ! ma Lou
LUI – Oh ! Marilou
Fais gaffe ou j'te rentre dans le chou

Paroles et musique Serge Gainsbourg
© 1977 by Melody Nelson Publishing

VARIATIONS SUR MARILOU — VARIATIONS ON MARILOU [1976]

The inimitable wordsmith at his very best. Gainsbourg sculpts his verses with ease and genius while artfully celebrating female masturbation. Each element of careful repetition is like a stroke of the poet's paintbrush as he unveils his verbal canvas. In the structure of the lyrics, here more than in any of his other songs, Gainsbourg's early training as a painter shines through.

In her absent gaze
And her absinthe iris
While Marilou amuses herself by
Blowing menthol smoke rings
Between two comic strip bubbles
All the while playing with the zipper
On her Levi's
I see vice
And it all reminds me of Carroll Lewis

In her absent gaze
And her absinthe iris
While Marilou does her best to
Blow smoke rings
Between two comic strip bubbles
All the while playing with her zipper
And cracking open her Levi's
In her empty gaze and her absinthe
Iris – as I was saying – I see vice
Proper to Baby Doll[124]
And it all reminds me of Lewis
Carroll

In her absent gaze
And her absinthe iris
While the speakers
Spit out
Quartal and quintal harmonies
Marilou ruins
Her health, killing herself
Just to get off

When Marilou vanishes
Into an absurd dream
And a coma envelops her
In obscure practices

---

124 Reference to Elia Kazan's 1956 film *Baby Doll* (screenplay by Tennessee Williams), which features a vacuous 19-year old woman who still dresses in young girls' clothes. The film was rather explicit in its sexual undertones, and efforts to ban it were undertaken.

VARIATIONS SUR MARILOU

Dans son regard absent
Et son iris absinthe
Tandis que Marilou s'amuse à faire des vol-
Utes de sèches au menthol
Entre deux bulles de comic strip
Tout en jouant avec le zip
De ses Levi's
Je lis le vice
Et je pense à Carroll Lewis

Dans son regard absent
Et son iris absinthe
Tandis que Marilou s'évertue à faire des vol-
Utes de sèches au menthol
Entre deux bulles de comic strip
Tout en jouant avec son zip
À entrebâiller ses Levi's
Dans son regard absent et son iris
Absinthe, dis-je, je lis le vice
De Baby Doll
Et je pense à Lewis
Carroll

Dans son regard absent
Et son iris absinthe
Quand crachent les enceintes
De la sono lançant
Accords de quartes et de quintes
Tandis que Marilou s'esquinte
La santé, s'éreinte
À s'envoyer en l'air

Lorsqu'en un songe absurde
Marilou se résorbe
Que son coma l'absorbe
En pratiques obscures

Her pupil grows absent
And her absinthe iris
Under the spell of her touch takes on
Hues of subliminal ecstasy
Vice lends her gaze
A salacious quality
A bit of the washed-out blue
Of her pair of Levi's
While she exhales
A menthol sigh
My little retard
Lost in exile
Both physical and mental
Plays with the metal
Of her zipper, and the coral
Atoll appears
She cozies up to it
A paused finger
On the edge of the corolla[125]
Is trapped next to the calyx[126]
That is Alice's rabbit hole
It all smacks of Lewis Carroll

When Marilou vanishes
Into obscure thoughts
And a coma envelops her
In absurd dreams
Her pupil grows absent
And her absinthe iris
Surreptitiously takes on
Hues of denied pleasure
Lost in exile
Both physical and mental
One by one she exhales
Feverish sighs
Infused with notes of menthol
My little retard
Plays notes on the metal
Of her zipper and, narcissistically
Delves further into vice
In the washed-out blue night
Of her pair of Levi's
Come to the pubic bone
Of her coral sex

---

125 Term used to designate the petals of a flower, when taken as a unit.

126 Term used to collectively designate the sepals of a flower. Usually green, sepals protect the flower in bud and help to support the petals when the flower is in bloom.

Sa pupille est absente
Et son iris absinthe
Sous ses gestes se teinte
D'extases sous-jacentes
À son regard le vice
Donne un côté salace
Un peu du bleu lavasse
De sa paire de Levi's
Tandis qu'elle exhale
Un soupir au menthol
Ma débile mentale
Perdue en son exil
Physique et cérébral
Joue avec le métal
De son zip, et l'atoll
De corail apparaît
Elle s'y coca-colle
Un doigt qui en arrêt
Au bord de la corolle
Est pris près du calice
Du vertige d'Alice
De Lewis Carroll

Lorsqu'en songes obscurs
Marilou se résorbe
Que son coma l'absorbe
En des rêves absurdes
Sa pupille s'absente
Et son iris absinthe
Subrepticement se teinte
De plaisirs en attente
Perdue dans son exil
Physique et cérébral
Un à un elle exhale
Des soupirs fébriles
Parfumés au menthol
Ma débile mentale
Fait tinter le métal
De son zip et, Narcisse
Elle pousse le vice
Dans la nuit bleu lavasse
De sa paire de Levi's
Arrivée au pubis
De son sexe corail

Spreading apart the corolla
Trapped at the edge
Of the calyx, Alice
Dives in to the bone
In the Evil-land
Of Lewis Carroll

Absent pupil, absinthe
Iris, Baby Doll
Listens to her idols
Jimi Hendrix, Elvis
Presley, T. Rex, Alice
Cooper, Lou Reed, The Roll-
Ing Stones, she's crazy about them
To that soundtrack, my Narcissus
Plunges with delight
Into the petrol blue night
Of her pair of Levi's
She comes to the pubic bone
And cool as menthol
She self-controls[127]
Her little orifice
Until, pushing vice
To the edge of the calyx
With one sex-symbol finger
Spreading apart her corolla
To a rock and roll soundtrack
My little Alice loses her way
In the Evil-land
Of Lewis Carroll

---

127 "Self-control" is in English in the original lyrics. Also used in *No comment* [1984].

Écartant la corolle
Prise au bord du calice
De vertigo, Alice
S'enfonce jusqu'à l'os
Au pays des malices
De Lewis Carroll

Pupille absente, iris
Absinthe, Baby Doll
Écoute ses idoles
Jimi Hendrix, Elvis
Presley, T. Rex, Alice
Cooper, Lou Reed, les Roll-
Ing Stones, elle en est folle
Là-dessus, cette Narcisse
Se plonge avec délice
Dans la nuit bleu pétrole
De sa paire de Levi's
Elle arrive au pubis
Et très cool au menthol
Elle se self-contrôle
Son petit orifice
Enfin, poussant le vice
Jusqu'au bord du calice
D'un doigt sex-symbole
S'écartant la corolle
Sur fond de rock'n'roll
S'égare mon Alice
Au pays des malices
De Lewis Carroll

Paroles et musique Serge Gainsbourg
© 1977 by Melody Nelson Publishing

MEURTRE À L'EXTINCTEUR — DEATH BY FIRE EXTINGUISHER [1976]

Marilou's murder, as narrated by its perpetrator.

To put out the fire in Marilou's ass
One evening, overcome with jealousy
I ran down the hotel hallway and brought back
The fire extinguisher

Brandishing the steel
Cylinder I hit her, BAM! and Marilou begins to groan
From her cracked skull leaks vermilion blood
Of a shade identical to that of the murder weapon

On the linoleum she has
One last spasm
One last tremor
I aim and fire, Marilou's body disappears under the foam

MEURTRE À L'EXTINCTEUR

Pour éteindre le feu au cul de Marilou
Un soir, n'en pouvant plus d'jalousie
J'ai couru au couloir de l'hôtel décrocher d'son clou
L'extincteur d'incendie

Brandissant le cylindre
D'acier je frappe, PAF ! et Marilou se met à geindre
De son crâne fendu s'échappe un sang vermeil
Identique au rouge sanglant d'l'appareil

Elle a sur le lino
Un dernier soubresaut
Une ultime secousse
J'appuie sur la manette, le corps de Marilou disparaît sous la mousse

Paroles et musique Serge Gainsbourg
© 1977 by Melody Nelson Publishing

MARILOU SOUS LA NEIGE — MARILOU UNDER THE SNOW [1976]

Our jilted lover's attempt at a eulogy for the woman who has driven him insane.* A most beautiful song.

> Marilou lies under the snow
> And I ask myself, over and over
> How I managed to corrupt the innocence
> Of all these childhood drawings
>
> Of my Lou in comic strips, I
> Traced the rounded bubbles' contours
> When I found myself excluded from her
> Erotic games, I fell ill over it[128]
>
> Marilou felt trapped
> Full or partial reproduction forbidden[129]
> As for my naïve self, I thought I'd be protected
> By the Opera Mundi copyrights[130]
>
> Oh! my Lou, I had to cut short
> Your existence, which is why
> Marilou is falling asleep under the snow
> The artificial snow of the fire extinguisher

---

128 For another example of a Gainsbourg protagonist "falling ill" over his love interest, see *L'hôtel particulier* [1971].

129 Note the subtle double meaning: on the one hand, Gainsbourg is riffing on the copyright theme. On the other, the line has very sexual undertones; Marilou obviously "[feels] trapped" in a mutually exclusive relationship and resents that her sexual freedoms ("reproduction" rights) are being curtailed.

130 Opera Mundi was a French media agency specializing in cartoon broadcasts. Famous American cartoons such as *Mickey Mouse* and *Felix the Cat*, which Gainsbourg grew up watching, would have borne Opera Mundi copyrights in France at the time. Marilou's jilted lover has clearly fallen prey to insanity: he believes Marilou is a comic strip character (noting her "rounded [speech] bubbles") and that his actions have been imaginary.

MARILOU SOUS LA NEIGE

Marilou repose sous la neige
Et je me dis, et je me redis
De tous ces dessins d'enfant, que n'ai-je
Pu préserver la fraîcheur de l'inédit

De ma Lou en bandes dessinées, je
Parcourais les bulles arrondies
Lorsque je me vis exclu de ses j-
Eux érotiques, j'en fis une maladie

Marilou se sentait prise au piège
Tous droits d'reproduction interdits
Moi, naïf, j'pensais que me protége-
Aient les droits du copyright Opéra Mundi

Oh ! Ma Lou, il fallait que j'abrège
Ton existence, c'est ainsi
Que Marilou s'endort sous la neige
Carbonique de l'extincteur d'incendie

Paroles et musique Serge Gainsbourg
© 1977 by Melody Nelson Publishing

LUNATIC ASYLUM [1976]

The final track off *L'Homme à tête de chou* finds our journalist committed to a mental institution. The eerily disjointed, often nonsensical lyrics reflect his current state of madness.

CHORISTS – Marilou, Marilou

HIM – The Playboy bunny
Gnaws at my vegetable brain
Shoe shine boy
Oh! Marilou, baby doll
You rolled me between thumb and forefinger like tobacco
You suckled me gently like a cachou[131]
And you spoke my language
Poo-poo-pee-doo[132]

You know, my Lou, in this white
Psychiatric ward
With much patience and dedication
I've managed to tame a cockchafer
So that it stands on my heliport head
The helicoleopter[133]
With its golden elytra[134]
Protec-
Ting the cockpit, lowers its antennae
Bearers of SOS signals, but shit, the geometer moths
Quivering with stress
Intercept my distress signals
In flight
I'm out of luck

CHORISTS – Marilou, Marilou

HIM – The Pou Radio parasites
Have scrambled my messages, crazy
As I was about you, Marilou

131   In English, "cachou" is a dated word meaning "lozenge". The original lyrics also use the word "cachou", which is a French brand of licorice-flavored breath mints.

132   Recalls similar onomatopoeia in *I Wanna Be Loved By You***, a song made timeless by Marilyn Monroe's rendition in Billy Wilder's 1959 film *Some Like it Hot*.

133   Helicoleopter = Helicopter + Coleoptera (order of insects commonly called beetles). The French dub this type of neologism – where two or more words are amalgamated to form another – a "mot-valise", meaning "suitcase-word". Perhaps the most famous example of a "mot-valise" in French literature is the "pianocktail" (piano + cocktail) dreamt up by Boris Vian in *L'écume des jours* (*Froth on the Daydream*). In this classic 1947 novel, the "pianocktail" refers to a modified piano that mixes drinks in accordance with the song being played on its keys; it is the main character's most prized possession. For more on Vian, see introductory notes to *Intoxicated Man* [1962].

134   Elytra are the protective, hardened forewings of beetles and certain other insect orders.

LUNATIC ASYLUM

Chœurs – Marilou, Marilou

Lui – Le petit lapin de "Playboy"
Ronge mon crâne végétal
Shoe shine boy
Oh ! Marilou, petit chou
Qui me roulait entre ses doigts comme du Caporal
Me suçotait comme un cachou
Et savait le dialecte chou
Poupouppidou

Tu sais, ma Lou, dans cette blanche clinique
Neuropsychiatrique
À force de patience et d'inaction
J'ai pu dresser un hanneton
Sur ma tête héliport
L'hélicoléoptère
De ses élytres d'or
Refer-
Mant l'habitacle, incline ses antennes
Porteuses d'SOS, mais merde, les phalènes
Frémissantes de stress
Interceptent en vol
Mes signaux de détresse
Manque de bol

Chœurs – Marilou, Marilou

Lui – Les parasites de radio Pou
Ont brouillé mes messages, fou
Que j'étais de toi, Marilou

Paroles et musique Serge Gainsbourg
© 1977 by Melody Nelson Publishing

SOFTCORE PORN AND A SUMMER DITTY

The year 1977 was the calm before the storm. Serge's last four records had been commercial failures, and he had yet to be rediscovered by an adoring, younger fan base. Serge spends most of his time writing songs for Jane Birkin's album *Ex-fan des sixties,* which would be a hit in 1978.

.

GOODBYE EMMANUELLE [1977]

This track was written for the soundtrack of Francois Leterrier's 1977 softcore porn film *Goodbye Emmanuelle,* the third installment in the rather successful *Emmanuelle* trilogy. Translated below is the album version, although the film version is very similar.

HER – Emmanuelle, Emmanuelle
Emmanuelle, goodbye
Emmanuelle, Emmanuelle
Emmanuelle, goodbye

Emmanuelle, Emmanuelle
Emmanuelle, goodbye
Emmanuelle, Emmanuelle
Emmanuelle, goodbye

HIM – *Emmanuelle loves*
Caresses both oral and manual
Emmanuelle loves
Collars both blue and white

Chorus

HIM – *Emmanuelle didn't learn*
How to love from books
Emmanuelle needs her
Annual dose of "I love you"

Chorus

HIM – *Emmanuelle loves*
Caresses both oral and manual
Emmanuelle loves
Collars both blue and white

GOODBYE EMMANUELLE

Elle – **Emmanuelle, Emmanuelle**
Emmanuelle, goodbye
Emmanuelle, Emmanuelle
Emmanuelle, goodbye

Emmanuelle, Emmanuelle
Emmanuelle, goodbye
Emmanuelle, Emmanuelle
Emmanuelle, goodbye

Lui – *Emmanuelle aime*
Les caresses buccales et manuelles
Emmanuelle aime
Les intellectuels et les manuels

Refrain

Lui – *Emmanuelle n'a pas a-*
Ppris à aimer dans les manuels
Emmanuelle a besoin de sa
Dose de "je t'aime" annuelle

Refrain

Lui – *Emmanuelle aime*
Les caresses buccales et manuelles
Emmanuelle aime
Les intellectuels et les manuels

Paroles Serge Gainsbourg
Musique Serge Gainsbourg & Jean-Pierre Sabard
© Melody Nelson Publishing/Trinacra Music

MY LADY HÉROÏNE – MY LADY HEROINE [1977]

This song finds Serge trying his hand at writing a summer hit.* He does so "just to make a buck, for fun."[135]

The song's melody is lifted from Albert Ketèlbey's *In a Persian Market.**

CHORISTS – Shala la, shala la
Shala la, shala la
Shala la, shala la
Shala la, shala lala lala la

Oh! my lady heroine
Oh! my lovely my goddess
Cradle me in your wings
My sweet angel, my beautiful

Oh! my lady heroine
My clandestine affair
Gently, my brown sugar[136]
Take me to heaven

CHORISTS – Shala la, shala la
Shala la, shala la
Shala la, shala la
Shala la, shala lala lala la

Oh! my lady heroine
Oh! my lovely my goddess
My platonic love
My baby, my only daughter[137]

Oh! my lady heroine
Pure as Justine[138]
All the misfortunes of your virtue
And all her gaieties are killing me

CHORISTS – Shala la
Shala la
Shala la

---

135 Gainsbourg, Verlant, **2000**, Albin Michel.

136 "Brown sugar" translates best as "cassonade" in French. Gainsbourg uses the term "sucre candi", which can also be brown in appearance. Regardless of the term used by the singer, his intent is obvious and the popular nickname for heroin is the only possible translation.

137 Charlotte was born to Serge and Jane Birkin in 1971, six years before this song was recorded. This couplet clearly foreshadows *Lemon Incest* [1984].**

138 *Justine, or the Misfortunes of Virtue* is a 1791 novel by the Marquis de Sade.**

MY LADY HÉROÏNE

CHŒURS – Shala la, shala la
Shala la, shala la
Shala la, shala la
Shala la, shala lala lala la

Oh ! my lady héroïne
Oh ! ma beauté ma divine
Referme sur moi tes ailes
Mon bel ange, ma toute belle

Oh ! my lady héroïne
Ma liaison clandestine
En douceur, mon sucre candi
Emmène-moi au paradis

CHŒURS – Shala la, shala la
Shala la, shala la
Shala la, shala la
Shala la, shala lala lala la

Oh ! my lady héroïne
Oh ! ma beauté ma divine
Toi mon amour platonique
Mon bébé, ma fille unique

Oh ! my lady héroïne
Aussi pure que Justine
Tous les malheurs de ta vertu
Et tous ses bonheurs me tuent

CHŒURS – Shala la
Shala la
Shala la

Shala la

Oh! my lady heroine
Within your beauty I can just make out
When your gaze cuts through me
All of Persia's delights

Oh! my lady heroin[139]
My opium, my cocaine
Do you hail from the Far East
Or from a Persian market?[140]

CHORISTS – Shala la, shala la
Shala la, shala la
Shala la, shala la
Shala la, shala lala lala la

CHORISTS – Shala la, shala la
Shala la, shala la
Shala la, shala la
Shala la, shala lala lala la

---

139 Up until this point, a blissfully innocent reader of the original lyrics could assume that Gainsbourg was truly serenading a female love interest, as the term "héroïne" means both "heroine" and "heroin" in French. However, our naïve reader would see their innocence shattered upon reading the verse immediately following the one to which this footnote is applied. Given that your translator did not have the luxury of working with such a brilliant homonym, a decision had to be made on when to drop the "e" and morph the female protagonist into a hard drug.

140 A coy nod to the man responsible for the song's melody.

Shala la

Oh ! my lady héroïne
Dans ta beauté je devine
Quand ton regard me transperce
Tous les charmes de la Perse

Oh ! my lady héroïne
Mon opium, ma cocaïne
Es-tu venue d'Extrême-Orient
Ou bien d'un marché persan

CHŒURS – Shala la, shala la
Shala la, shala la
Shala la, shala la
Shala la, shala lala lala la

CHŒURS – Shala la, shala la
Shala la, shala la
Shala la, shala la
Shala la, shala lala lala la

AUX ARMES ET CÆTERA

Toward the end of 1978, Philips Records puts out a series of anthology albums to mark Serge's twentieth year in show business. A younger generation begins to take interest in the early classics and rediscovers the commercially unsuccessful concept albums of the 70's. Gainsbourg's past begins to place his star on this rise, but a fresh album is needed to stay relevant and capitalize on the newfound popularity brought on by his old hits.

In early 1979, Gainsbourg records his reggae-infused record *Aux armes et cætera* in Jamaica at Kingston's famous Dynamic Sounds studio. He makes history as the first white artist to record there; Bob Dylan, Ian Dury, and Joe Cocker would all follow in his footsteps. Bob Marley's wife, Rita Marley, even provides backup vocals for the album. Upon arriving at Dynamic Sounds, the musicians inform Serge that they only know one French song: an old hit called *Je t'aime moi non plus*.* One can only imagine the scene when Serge let them in on his identity.

The album is perhaps most famous for its title track, a reggae rendition of *La Marseillaise* (the French national anthem) which outraged conservatives. A columnist named Michel Droit even went so far as to declare that Gainsbourg was bringing anti-semitism upon himself and all his fellow Jews by supposedly defiling *La Marseillaise,* "the most sacred [of our nation's treasures]".

Six months after the album's release, on December 22nd, 1979, Serge gave his first concert in fifteen years, at *Le Palace* in Paris. As *Aux Armes et caetera* proceeded to go gold and then platinum, Serge went on tour, stopping in Strasbourg in early January, 1980. At the city's concert hall, he was confronted by an angry group of soldiers from a nearby base who threatened to come to blows with him if he dared to sing his version of the national anthem. Terrified, his Jamaican musicians refused to go on stage. With great composure and amidst loud jeering from the crowd, Gainsbourg declared that he was being forced to cancel the concert due to the presence of belligerent "far-right groups". He then asked the crowd to sing along with him as he belted out the anthem's first stanza, *a cappella* and with no hint of reggae intonation. After a few moments of indecisiveness, the soldiers eventually stood at attention and sang along. Serge punctuated the performance with a heartfelt *bras d'honneur* before storming off the stage, his career now stronger than ever and his anti-conformist legacy secure.

On December 14th, 1981, Serge purchased the original manuscript of *La Marseillaise* at auction for 135,000 francs (about $70,000 in 2020 dollars). *"I was prepared to go bankrupt for this",* he would say immediately following the purchase. Why such determination? *La Marseillaise's* composer, Rouget de Lisle, had not re-written the chorus in its entirety after each successive stanza. Rather, he had shortened it to "Aux armes, citoyens! etc.", thereby vindicating Serge and his "shortcut" of an album title.

BRIGADE DES STUPS — NARCOTICS DIVISION [1979]

An homage to Serge's neighborhood's policemen, who always treated him well even as his behavior became increasingly erratic.

At the narcotics division
I was handed to a bunch of cops
They searched me for a spliff
Instead they found my dick

At the narcotics division
There's an old seadog
Who's completely bats
Always half smashed

At the narcotics division
Everyone's fixated on drugs
I'm scared, I'm flipping out
Really not my kind of trip

At the narcotics division
What they wanted was a scoop
Now here comes the old seadog
Asking me for an autograph

At the narcotics division
I tell them I only smoke cigs
I'm the cinematograph's[141]
Betty Boop[142]

---

141   A cinematograph is a motion picture film camera and projector. Invented in France in the 1890's, it is commonly associated with the birth of cinema.

142   Betty Boop is an animated cartoon character created by Max Fleischer (1883-1972), who was also the man responsible for bringing iconic characters such as Popeye and Superman to the silver screen. Modeled off the Jazz Age flappers and singer Helen Kane, Betty Boop is often considered to be the first animated sex symbol.

BRIGADE DES STUPS

À la brigade des stups
J'suis tombé sur des cops
Ils ont cherché mon spliff
Ils ont trouvé mon paf

À la brigade des stups
Y'a un ancien mataf
Qu'est complètement louf
Toujours à moitié paf

À la brigade des stups
Idée fixe la chnouf
J'ai les moules, je flippe
C'est pas mon genre de trip

À la brigade des stups
C'qu'ils voulaient c'est un scoop
V'là que l'ancien mataf
M'demande un autographe

À la brigade des stups
J'leur dis "J'fume que les Troupes"
Je suis la Betty Boop
Du cinématographe

Paroles et musique Serge Gainsbourg
© 1979 Melody Nelson Publishing

ENTER GAINSBARRE:
TO SYNTHS, AFROBEAT, AND FUNK

In early 1980, Serge is a bona fide superstar. He is now his label's top-selling recording artist, having vaulted past rocker Johnny Halliday. However, the bottle is rapidly turning him into Gainsbarre, a mercurial, brooding, and abusive alter ego. Asked to explain the Gainsbourg/Gainsbarre duality, he would later declare: *"Gainsbourg se barre quand Gainsbarre se bourre",* meaning *"When Gainsbarre gets drunk, Gainsbourg gets lost."* A passage from Verlant's biography: "When she comes home from school, Kate Barry, 13, never knows what to expect – the 50-year-old child who jokes around and plays games with her and Charlotte, or that 'frightening person who was brutal and harsh with his words.'"[143]

Mid-September, 1980. Jane leaves Serge. "In the alcoholic Gainsbarre, [Jane] no longer sees any trace of the Gainsbourg she once loved [...]. Everything happens very quickly, very brutally. Jane tells [Kate and Charlotte] to pack their bags. Distraught, she joins Serge in the kitchen to talk, swearing that she loves him passionately, that she wants to stay, that she doesn't think she can make it without him. She remembers him looking like a little kid who couldn't understand the seriousness of his deeds."[144]

Serge had mistreated Jane for too long, both verbally and physically, and confessed as much. *"It's my fault that Jane left. I abused her too much. I'd come home completely hammered, I would hit her. I didn't like it when she yelled at me: a few seconds too long and wham... She put up with a lot [...]."*[145] *Sorry Angel* [1984] offers further musings on the breakup.

Serge's nightclub-entrepreneur friend Régine: *"Serge caused the break-up. He wanted it and he planned it. He could never forgive her for having considered a romance with someone else. When she left, he told me he'd never take her back."*[146] Régine is referring to Jacques Doillon, a filmmaker who had offered Jane the leading role in *La fille prodigue.* Jane gave birth to Lou Doillon on September 4th, 1982.

143 Gainsbourg, Verlant, **2000**, Albin Michel.
144 Gainsbourg, Verlant, **2000**, Albin Michel.
145 Gainsbourg in Time, Verlant, **February 2001**, Gala Magazine.
146 Gainsbourg, Verlant, **2000**, Albin Michel.

Gainsbourg would record three more albums – *Mauvaises nouvelles des étoiles, Love on the beat, and You're under arrest* – before his death on March 2nd, 1991. Serge died painlessly, of cardiac arrest. No doubt the ghost of Charlie the Twist Dancer basked in the irony.[147]

---

147 See *Requiem pour un twisteur* [1962].

DIEU FUMEUR DE HAVANES – GOD THE CUBAN CIGAR SMOKER [1980]

The inspiration for this song came during a transatlantic flight on the Concorde; Serge imagined that the clouds he was seeing from the window were the result of God's smoking habit. Serge would go on to compose an entire album (*Souviens-toi de m'oublier*) for Catherine Deneuve, with whom he sang this duet.*

HIM – God is a Cuban cigar smoker
I see his gray clouds
I know he even smokes at night
Just as I do my dear

HER – You're nothing but a Gitanes[148] smoker
I see your blue smoke rings
At times bringing tears to my eyes
You are my master after God

HIM – God is a Cuban cigar smoker
He himself told me
That smoke sends one to heaven
I know it my dear

HER – You're nothing but a Gitanes smoker
Without them you are unhappy
Open your eyes in the moonlight
For the love of God

HIM – God is a Cuban cigar smoker
Close to you far from him
I'd like to keep you my entire life
Please understand my dear

HER – You're nothing but a Gitanes smoker
And I want to see the last one
Shine deep within my eyes
Love me for God's sake

HIM – God is a Cuban cigar smoker
Close to you far from him
I'd like to keep you my entire life
Please understand my dear

HER – You're nothing but a Gitanes smoker
And I want to see the last one
Shine deep within my eyes

---

148 Gitanes was the French brand of cigarettes favored by Serge, who was known to smoke three packs a day.

DIEU FUMEUR DE HAVANES

Lui – Dieu est un fumeur de havanes
Je vois ses nuages gris
Je sais qu'il fume même la nuit
Comme moi ma chérie

Elle – Tu n'es qu'un fumeur de gitanes
Je vois tes volutes bleues
M'faire parfois venir les larmes aux yeux
Tu es mon maître après Dieu

Lui – Dieu est un fumeur de havanes
C'est lui-même qui m'a dit
Que la fumée envoie au paradis
Je le sais ma chérie

Elle – Tu n'es qu'un fumeur de gitanes
Sans elles tu es malheureux
Au clair de la lune ouvre les yeux
Pour l'amour de Dieu

Lui – Dieu est un fumeur de havanes
Tout près de toi loin de lui
J'aimerais te garder toute ma vie
Comprends-moi ma chérie

Elle – Tu n'es qu'un fumeur de gitanes
Et la dernière je veux
La voir briller au fond de mes yeux
Aime-moi nom de Dieu

Lui – Dieu est un fumeur de havanes
Tout près de toi loin de lui
J'aimerais te garder toute ma vie
Comprends-moi ma chérie

Elle – Tu n'es qu'un fumeur de gitanes
Et la dernière je veux
La voir briller au fond de mes yeux

Love me for God's sake

Aime-moi nom de Dieu

Paroles et musique Serge Gainsbourg
© Pathé Productions

ECCE HOMO [1981]

This is the first and only song to mention Gainsbourg's alter ego, Gainsbarre, thus completing the transformation foreshadowed by *Docteur Jekyll et Monsieur Hyde* [1966].

Ecce Homo is off *Mauvaises nouvelles des étoiles,* the first Gainsbourg album to come out after his breakup with Jane Birkin.

CHORISTS – Ecce homo, ecce homo[149]
Ecce homo, ecce homo, homo, homo
Ecce homo, ecce homo
Ecce homo, ecce homo

HIM – Yep! I'm Gainsbarre
I can always be found
In nightclubs and American
Bars, I have a swell time there[150]

Chorus

HIM – Gainsbarre's signature style
Features blue jeans, three-night
Stubble, cigars
And bouts of depression

Chorus

HIM – Gainsbarre is bizarre
He's cool, it's as though
He doesn't give a damn about
Anything, well, maybe not quite

Chorus

HIM – Yep! Crucified was Gainsbarre
On Golgothar[151]
He's a reggae-man, ecstatic
His heart pierced through and through

---

149 Pontius Pilate's infamous words as he presented a scourged Jesus Christ to the crowd shortly before his crucifixion. They are often translated as: "Behold the man."

150 The original lyrics read "c'est bonnard", which has been translated as "I have a swell time there". "Bonnard" is an obsolete adjective meaning "nice, satisfying". However, given the self-descriptive, pictorial nature of the song, the line could also be a veiled reference to Pierre Bonnard, a French painter (1867-1947) most famous for his domestic scenes.**

151 Golgotha is the site outside Jerusalem where Jesus was crucified. Gainsbourg adds an "r" at the end of the word to make it rhyme with "Gainsbarre".

ECCE HOMO

CHŒURS – **Ecce homo, ecce homo**
Ecce homo, ecce homo, homo, homo
Ecce homo, ecce homo
Ecce homo, ecce homo

LUI – Eh ! ouais, c'est moi Gainsbarre
On me trouve au hasard
Des night-clubs et des bars
Américains c'est bonnard

Refrain

LUI – On reconnaît Gainsbarre
À ses jeans, à sa bar-
Be de trois nuits, ses cigares
Et ses coups de cafard

Refrain

LUI – Bizarre, ce Gainsbarre
Il est cool, faut croire
Que de tout il en arre
Ien à cirer, enfin, faut voir

Refrain

LUI – Eh ! ouais, cloué le Gainsbarre
Au mont du Golgothar
Il est reggae, hilare
Le cœur percé de part en part

Chorus x2

Ecce homo

Refrain bissé

Ecce homo

Paroles et musique Serge Gainsbourg
© 1982 by Melody Nelson Publishing

LA NOSTALGIE CAMARADE — NOSTALGIA COMRADE [1981]

In 1980, Gainsbourg met twenty-one-year-old model Caroline Paulus (aka Bambou) at *L'Élysée-Matignon*, a Paris nightclub. In a 2001 interview published by the French magazine *Les Inrocks*, Bambou recalled their first encounter:

"It was quite simple: I called him an old asshole, he called me an ugly lard-ass, and we both cracked up. It was at L'Élysée-Matignon, I was dancing and the club's owner comes up to me and says 'Mr. Gainsbourg orders you to come to his table'. I said 'What! That old asshole! He can go fuck himself.' I went back to my table and he came over, staggering about, champagne bucket in hand, and told me 'The old asshole is coming to your table, you ugly lard-ass.'"

Bambou was the fruit of a union between an aristocratic Sino-Vietnamese woman and a German member of the French Foreign Legion. Bambou's father fought in France's Indochina War (1945-1954)*, which could be the theme of this song.

Bambou would stay with Serge until his death in 1991. The couple had one child together (Lucien, or Lulu, born in 1986).

HIM – *What the hell were you thinking when you tore down that savage's*
Hut, and then when you took out your pocketknife
And disemboweled the primitive
Who had just emerged from the brush

CHORISTS – Nostalgia comrade
Nostalgia comrade
Nostalgia comrade
Nostalgia comrade

HIM – *What made you take that diaphanous girl*
Against her will as she clawed away at you
Any regrets, you say negative
You even snicker about it

Chorus

HIM – *What makes you drink sugarcane*
Until you're smashed, until you founder on the reef
Of your memory and see your passive past
As you get high on rosin

Chorus

HIM – *So many things happen in that shaved*
Head of yours, it's full of sadness and hash
You still see yourself in explosive-laden jungle camo
Jumping from your airplane

LA NOSTALGIE CAMARADE

Lui – *Qu'est-ce qui t'a pris bordel de casser la cabane*
De ce panoupanou, puis sortir ton canif
Ouvrir le bide au primitif
Qui débarquait de sa savane

Chœurs – **La nostalgie camarade**
La nostalgie camarade
La nostalgie camarade
La nostalgie camarade

Lui – *Qu'est-ce qui t'a fait prendre cette fille diaphane*
Contre son gré et sous ses griffes
Des regrets, tu réponds négatif
Mieux encore tu ricanes

Refrain

Lui – *Qu'est-ce qui te prend au sucre de canne*
De te klaxonner la gueule, sombrer sur les récifs
De ta mémoire et revoir ton passif
En respirant la colophane

Refrain

Lui – *Il s'en passe des choses sous ton crâne*
Rasé, c'est plein de tristesse et de kif
Tu t'vois encore en tenue léopard bourrée d'explosifs
Sauter de ton aéroplane

Chorus

CHORISTS – Comrade
Comrade
Comrade
Comrade

Chorus x2

Refrain

Chœurs – Camarade
Camarade
Camarade
Camarade

Refrain bissé

Paroles et musique Serge Gainsbourg
© 1982 by Melody Nelson Publishing

BANA BASADI BALALO [1981]

Set to reggae music, this song tells the story of three young Zulus as they valiantly resist the Boers' colonization of South Africa.

> CHORISTS – Bana basadi balalo
> HIM – Bantu dialect[152]
> CHORISTS – Bana basadi balalo
> HIM – Three little Zulus
> CHORISTS – Bana basadi balalo
> HIM – Went to war
> CHORISTS – Bana basadi balalo
> HIM – Against the Boers
>
> CHORISTS – Bana basadi balalo
> HIM – Bantu dialect
> CHORISTS – Bana basadi balalo
> HIM – Three little Zulus
> CHORISTS – Bana basadi balalo
> HIM – Kill the Dutchman
> CHORISTS – Bana basadi balalo
> HIM – With spears
>
> CHORISTS – Bana basadi balalo
> HIM – Bantu dialect
> CHORISTS – Bana basadi balalo
> HIM – Three little Zulus
> CHORISTS – Bana basadi balalo
> Bana basadi balalo
> Bana basadi balalo
> Bana basadi balalo
>
> CHORISTS – Bana basadi balalo
> HIM – Bantu dialect
> CHORISTS – Bana basadi balalo
> HIM – Three little Zulus
> CHORISTS – Bana basadi balalo
> HIM – Three little Negroes
> CHORISTS – Bana basadi balalo
> HIM – Died as heroes
>
> CHORISTS – Bana basadi balalo
> Bana basadi balalo
> Bana basadi balalo
> Bana basadi balalo

---

152 "Bantu" is an umbrella term used to designate hundreds of mutually intelligible dialects spoken mostly in Central, Southeastern, and Southern Africa. Zulu is one such language.

BANA BASADI BALALO

CHŒURS – Bana basadi balalo
LUI – Dialecte bantou
CHŒURS – Bana basadi balalo
LUI – Trois petits zoulous
CHŒURS – Bana basadi balalo
LUI – Sont partis en guerre
CHŒURS – Bana basadi balalo
LUI – Contre les Boers

CHŒURS – Bana basadi balalo
LUI – Dialecte bantou
CHŒURS – Bana basadi balalo
LUI – Trois petits zoulous
CHŒURS – Bana basadi balalo
LUI – Tuent à la sagaie
CHŒURS – Bana basadi balalo
LUI – Le Néerlandais

CHŒURS – Bana basadi balalo
LUI – Dialecte bantou
CHŒURS – Bana basadi balalo
LUI – Trois petits zoulous
CHŒURS – Bana basadi balalo
Bana basadi balalo
Bana basadi balalo
Bana basadi balalo

CHŒURS – Bana basadi balalo
LUI – Dialecte bantou
CHŒURS – Bana basadi balalo
LUI – Trois petits zoulous
CHŒURS – Bana basadi balalo
LUI – Trois petits négros
CHŒURS – Bana basadi balalo
LUI – Sont morts en héros

CHŒURS – Bana basadi balalo
Bana basadi balalo
Bana basadi balalo
Bana basadi balalo

Bana basadi balalo
Bana basadi balalo
Bana basadi balalo
Bana basadi balalo

Bana basadi balalo
Bana basadi balalo
Bana basadi balalo
Bana basadi balalo

Paroles et musique Serge Gainsbourg
© 1982 by Melody Nelson Publishing

LOVE ON THE BEAT [1984]

The title and opening track off this sexually explicit album, which cemented Serge's comeback by earning platinum certification in France. Employing a heavy dose of synthesizers and funk rock, the record explores love and sex of many brands: heterosexual (*Love on the Beat, No Comment*), homosexual (*Kiss Me Hardy, I'm the Boy*), and even incestuous (*Lemon Incest*). The album cover shows a shirtless Serge in heavy makeup, holding a cigarette just so.

This offering marks a clear departure from the reggae style that had defined Serge's two prior records. This eight-minute opening song, with its backing track composed exclusively of Bambou's[153] tortured screams of pleasure, sets the tone from the outset.

CHORISTS – Love on the beat[154]
Love on the beat

HIM – First I want with my mother
Tongue to read your mind
But you're already, you're already listing
On the flux and reflux of the tide

Chorus

HIM – I have you in my sights
My spread-eagled, lovely child
There, I've touched the sensitive spot
Wait, while I dwell on it

Chorus

HIM – It's time to move on to more serious
Things, my pretty doll
You desire a fucking
Overdose, there you go, I'm inside you

CHORISTS – Love on the beat
Love on the beat, beat, beat, beat

Chorus

HIM – I quite enjoy your purring
Your claws out, my teeth sunk in
Your nape, watching while ruby pearls

---

153 For more on Bambou, see introductory notes to *La nostalgie camarade* [1981].

154 A French person would pronounce the English word "beat" and the French word "bite" exactly the same way. Note that "bite" is slang for "penis" in French, the same way "cock" is in English, thereby adding a degree of innuendo to the album title.

LOVE ON THE BEAT

CHŒURS – Love on the beat
Love on the beat

Lui – *D'abord je veux avec ma langue*
Natale deviner tes pensées
Mais toi déjà, déjà tu tangues
Aux flux et reflux des marées

Refrain

Lui – *Je pense à toi en tant que cible*
Ma belle enfant écartelée
Là, j'ai touché le point sensible
Attends, je vais m'y attarder

Refrain

Lui – *Il est temps de passer aux choses*
Sérieuses, ma poupée jolie
Tu as envie d'une overdose
De baise, voilà, je m'introduis

CHŒURS – Love on the beat
Love on the beat, beat, beat, beat

Refrain

Lui – *J'aime assez tes miaou-miaous*
Griffes dehors, moi dents dedans
Ta nuque, voir de ton joli cou

Of blood form on your pretty neck

Chorus

HIM – The more you scream, the deeper I'll go
As I sink into your stirring
Quicksand[155] *I shall tell you*
The most abominable things

CHORISTS – Love... – I said "You Love"... – On the beat
Love... – I said "I want your love"... – On the on the beat, beat

Love on the beat
Love on the beat, beat, beat, beat

HIM – Your orifices are all scalding
Of the three the gods gave you
I've chosen the least smooth one
For the culmination, my finale

Chorus

HIM – A six-thousand volt shock
Has just spurted out of my pylon
And our loins find themselves stricken
With a case of synchronized epilepsy

CHORISTS – Love on the beat
Love, love, love, love, love, love on the beat

Love... – Love baby... – On the beat
Love on the, on the beat

Love on the beat
Love on the beat

Love on the beat
Love, love, love, love on the beat

---

155 The French words for "quicksand" are "sables mouvants". Literally translated, this means "moving sand". Also, the French word for "moving" – as in "producing emotion" – is "émouvant". Gainsbourg exploits this similarity by modifying the French term for quicksand so that it reads "sables émouvants", or "emotion-producing sand". This novel way of describing an aroused vagina has been (somewhat disappointingly) translated as "stirring quicksand".

Comme un rubis perler le sang

Refrain

LUI – *Plus tu cries, plus profond j'irai*
Dans tes sables émouvants, sables
Où m'enlisant je te dirai
Les mots les plus abominables

CHŒURS – Love… – I said "You Love"… – On the beat
Love… – I said "I want your love"… – On the on the beat, beat

Love on the beat
Love on the beat, beat, beat, beat

LUI – *Brûlants sont tous tes orifices*
Des trois que les dieux t'ont donnés
Je décide dans le moins lisse
D'achever, de m'abandonner

Refrain

LUI – *Une décharge de six mille volts*
Vient de gicler de mon pylône
Et nos reins alors se révoltent
D'un coup d'épilepsie synchrone

CHŒURS – Love on the beat
Love, love, love, love, love, love on the beat

Love… – Love baby… – On the beat
Love on the, on the beat

Love on the beat
Love on the beat

Love on the beat
Love, love, love, love on the beat

Paroles et musique Serge Gainsbourg
© 1984 Melody Nelson Publishing

SORRY ANGEL [1984]

Sorry Angel finds Serge reflecting on his painful breakup with Jane Birkin. Appearing very conflicted, he apologizes repeatedly in the chorus, only to also state that he has "neither remorse, nor regrets".*

CHORISTS – Sorry angel
Sorry so
Sorry angel
Sorry so[156]

HIM – *I am the one who suicided you*
My love
I wasn't worth it
You know
Without me you decided
One fine day
Decided you were leaving

Chorus

HIM – *The count had started*
Down
Was it vertigo, or bad luck
Who knows
A trip, only one-way
It runs long
And one never comes back from it

Chorus

HIM – *Me, I would have tried anything*
My love
It really wasn't worth it
I know
That it was doomed from the start
My love
I have neither remorse, nor regrets

Chorus

HIM – *I am the one who suicided you*
My love
I am the one who slit your wrists
I know
You are now among the angels

---

156   The chorus is in English in the original lyrics.

SORRY ANGEL

Chœurs – Sorry angel
Sorry so
Sorry angel
Sorry so

Lui – C'est moi qui t'ai suicidée
Mon amour
Je n'en valais pas la peine
Tu sais
Sans moi tu as décidé
Un beau jour
Décidé que tu t'en allais

Refrain

Lui – Le compte avait commencé
À rebours
Était-ce vertige, déveine
Qui sait
Un voyage, un seul aller
Au long cours
D'où l'on ne revient jamais

Refrain

Lui – Moi, j'aurai tout essayé
Mon amour
C'était vraiment pas la peine
Je sais
Que c'était foutu d'avance
Mon amour
J'n'ai ni remords, ni regret

Refrain

Lui – C'est moi qui t'ai suicidée
Mon amour
Moi qui t'ai ouvert les veines
Je sais
Maintenant tu es avec les anges

Forever
Forever and always

Chorus x2

HIM – *I am the one who suicided you*
My love
I am the one who slit your wrists
I know
You are now amidst the angels
Forever
Forever and always

Chorus x3

Pour toujours
Pour toujours et à jamais

Refrain bissé

LUI – C'est moi qui t'ai suicidée
Mon amour
Moi qui t'ai ouvert les veines
Je sais
Maintenant tu es avec les anges
Pour toujours
Pour toujours et à jamais

Refrain trissé

Paroles et musique Serge Gainsbourg
© 1984 by Melody Nelson Publishing

NO COMMENT [1984]

Incendiary lyrics set to rather pedestrian music. The strength of this song lies in the contrast between the mellifluous pseudo-detachment of the chorists and the brash sexuality of the male voice.

CHORISTS – Ooh, ooh, ooh!
No comment
Ooh, ooh, ooh!
No comment

CHORISTS – Ooh, ooh, ooh!
HIM – *Have I got what, affirmative, and what else now...*
CHORISTS – No comment
HIM – *Do I fuck, affirmative, what, you want names...*
CHORISTS – No comment
HIM – *Sluts, affirmative, actresses...*
CHORISTS – No comment
HIM – *Young girls, affirmative, how old...*
CHORISTS – Ooh, ooh, ooh!

CHORISTS – Ooh, ooh, ooh!
HIM – *Have I got what, affirmative, and what else now...*
CHORISTS – No comment
HIM – *Do I get hard, affirmative, for whom...*
CHORISTS – No comment
HIM – *For whores, affirmative, and for whom else...*
CHORISTS – No comment
HIM – *Brunettes, blondes, affirmative, and redheads...*
CHORISTS – Ooh, ooh, ooh!

CHORISTS – Ooh, ooh, ooh!
HIM – *Have I got what, affirmative, and what else now...*
CHORISTS – No comment
HIM – *Am I a good lay, affirmative, what, alone...*
CHORISTS – No comment
HIM – *Technique, affirmative, skilled with my fingers...*
CHORISTS – No comment
HIM – *Self-control, affirmative, how so...*[157]
CHORISTS – Ooh, ooh, ooh!

CHORISTS – Ooh, ooh, ooh!
HIM – *Have I got what, affirmative, and what else now...*
CHORISTS – No comment
HIM – *Do I like it, affirmative, which side...*

---

157 "Self-control" is in English in the original lyrics. The same word is used in the epic *Variations sur Marilou* [1976].

NO COMMENT

CHŒURS – Ooh, ooh, ooh !
No comment
Ooh, ooh, ooh !
No comment

CHŒURS – Ooh, ooh, ooh !
LUI – *Si j'ai quoi, affirmatif, et quoi d'autre...*
CHŒURS – No comment
LUI – *Si je baise, affirmatif, quoi des noms...*
CHŒURS – No comment
LUI – *Des salopes, affirmatif, des actrices...*
CHŒURS – No comment
LUI – *Des gamines, affirmatif, de quel âge...*
CHŒURS – Ooh, ooh, ooh !

CHŒURS – Ooh, ooh, ooh !
LUI – *Si j'ai quoi, affirmatif, et quoi d'autre...*
CHŒURS – No comment
LUI – *Si je bande, affirmatif, pour qui ça...*
CHŒURS – No comment
LUI – *Pour des putes, affirmatif, et qui d'autre...*
CHŒURS – No comment
LUI – *Brunes, blondes, affirmatif, et rouquines...*
CHŒURS – Ooh, ooh, ooh !

CHŒURS – Ooh, ooh, ooh !
LUI – *Si j'ai quoi, affirmatif, et quoi d'autre...*
CHŒURS – No comment
LUI – *Si j'assure, affirmatif, quoi, tout seul...*
CHŒURS – No comment
LUI – *D'la technique, affirmatif, du doigté...*
CHŒURS – No comment
LUI – *Self-control, affirmatif, comment ça...*
CHŒURS – Ooh, ooh, ooh !

CHŒURS – Ooh, ooh, ooh !
LUI – *Si j'ai quoi, affirmatif, et quoi d'autre...*
CHŒURS – No comment
LUI – *Si j'aime ça, affirmatif, quel côté...*

CHORISTS – No comment

HIM – *My preferences, affirmative, are of little importance...*
CHORISTS – No comment
HIM – *Addicted, affirmative, to sex...*
CHORISTS – Ooh, ooh, ooh!

CHORISTS – Ooh, ooh, ooh!

HIM – *Have I got what, affirmative, and what else now...*
CHORISTS – No comment
HIM – *Am I a good lay, affirmative, what, alone...*
CHORISTS – No comment
HIM – *Technique, affirmative, skilled with my fingers...*
CHORISTS – No comment
HIM – *Self-control, affirmative, how so...*
CHORISTS – Ooh, ooh, ooh!

CHORISTS – Ooh, ooh, ooh!
HIM – *Have I got what, affirmative, and what else now...*
CHORISTS – No comment
HIM – *Do I like it, affirmative, which side...*
CHORISTS – No comment
HIM – *My preferences, affirmative, are of little importance...*
CHORISTS – No comment
HIM – *Addicted, affirmative, to sex...*
CHORISTS – Ooh, ooh, ooh!

CHORISTS – Ooh, ooh, ooh!
No comment
No comment
No comment
Ooh, ooh, ooh!

CHORISTS – Ooh, ooh, ooh!
No comment
No comment
No comment
Ooh, ooh, ooh!

CHORISTS – Ooh, ooh, ooh!
No comment
No comment
No comment
Ooh, ooh, ooh!

CHŒURS – No comment

LUI – *Peu importe, affirmatif, c'que j'préfère...*
CHŒURS – No comment
LUI – *Obsédé, affirmatif, sexuel...*
CHŒURS – Ooh, ooh, ooh !

CHŒURS – Ooh, ooh, ooh !

LUI – *Si j'ai quoi, affirmatif, et quoi d'autre...*
CHŒURS – No comment
LUI – *Si j'assure, affirmatif, quoi, tout seul...*
CHŒURS – No comment
LUI – *D'la technique, affirmatif, du doigté...*
CHŒURS – No comment
LUI – *Self-control, affirmatif, comment ça...*
CHŒURS – Ooh, ooh, ooh !

CHŒURS – Ooh, ooh, ooh !
LUI – *Si j'ai quoi, affirmatif, et quoi d'autre...*
CHŒURS – No comment
LUI – *Si j'aime ça, affirmatif, quel côté...*
CHŒURS – No comment
LUI – *Peu m'importe, affirmatif, c'que j'préfère...*
CHŒURS – No comment
LUI – *Obsédé, affirmatif, sexuel...*
CHŒURS – Ooh, ooh, ooh !

CHŒURS – Ooh, ooh, ooh !
No comment
No comment
No comment
Ooh, ooh, ooh !

CHŒURS – Ooh, ooh, ooh !
No comment
No comment
No comment
Ooh, ooh, ooh !

CHŒURS – Ooh, ooh, ooh !
No comment
No comment
No comment
Ooh, ooh, ooh !

Paroles et musique Serge Gainsbourg
© 1984 by Melody Nelson Publishing

LEMON INCEST [1984]

For obvious reasons, this duet with thirteen-year-old Charlotte Gainsbourg was and remains one of Serge's most controversial songs. The music video shows the two of them lying in an oversized black leather bed; Charlotte is wearing nothing but panties and a pajama top, while her father wears only pants. The singer was always careful to dispel rumors about his relationship with Charlotte while also managing to stoke the fire of scandal. He famously said: *"L'inceste, je l'ai effleuré. Point. Pas défloré."***, which translates as: *"I flirted with incest. Period. I did not deflower it"*.

The song is set to Chopin's *Étude no. 3 in E major Opus 10*.

> **HER – Inceste de citron**
> **CHORISTS – Lemon incest**[158]
> **HER – I love you, love you, I love you more than anything**
> **CHORISTS - Papapappa**[159]
> **HIM – Naïve as an Henri Rousseau**[160] **canvas**
> **Your kisses are so sweet**
> **HER – Inceste de citron**
> **CHORISTS – Lemon incest**
> **HER - I love you, love you, I love you more than anything**
> **CHORISTS - Papapappa**
>
> HER – The love we'll never make together
> Is the most beautiful, the most violent
> The purest, the headiest
> HIM – Exquisite silhouette[161], luscious child
> My flesh and blood
> Oh! my baby, my soul[162]

---

158 The opening two verses have not been translated. Had the first verse been translated to English, it would have read "lemon incest", causing an unfortunate redundancy. The second verse requires no translation as it is sung in English. Note the subtle wordplay: "inceste de citron" sounds very much like "un zeste de citron", meaning "a zest of lemon".

159 Note the clever use of the "lalala" structure. "Papa" is what children call their fathers in France; its equivalent in English would be "Dad" or "Daddy".

160 Gainsbourg's lyrics refer to Henri Rousseau as "Nierdoi Sseaurou". A common practice in French slang is to invert the order of syllables; this is called "verlan" (a designation that is itself a syllabic inversion of the French "à l'envers", meaning "backwards"). Re-establishing the correct syllabic order on "Nierdoi Sseaurou" yields "Douanier Rousseau". Henri Rousseau was a 19th century French painter who had been a tax collector before devoting himself entirely to his art, earning the nickname "douanier" (meaning "customs officer") along the way.** He is considered one of the leading figures of the Naïve art movement, a detail that ties in seamlessly with Gainsbourg's choice of adjective for his daughter.

161 "Exquise esquisse" translates literally as "exquisite outline" or "exquisite sketch". However, these translation options lack the formidable alliteration and precise syllable count present in the original. Your translator felt that "exquisite silhouette" conserved some of these properties while still remaining rather true to the original meaning.

162 Gainsbourg was inspired by the opening lines of Nabokov's *Lolita*: "Lolita, light of my life, fire of my loins. My sin, my soul."** Note that Gainsbourg made certain not to include the word "sin" in his song.

LEMON INCEST

ELLE – **Inceste de citron**
CHŒURS – **Lemon incest**
ELLE – **Je t'aime, t'aime, je t'aime plus que tout**
CHŒURS – **Papapappa**
LUI – **Naïve comme une toile du Nierdoi Sseaurou**
Tes baisers sont si doux
ELLE – **Inceste de citron**
CHŒURS – **Lemon incest**
ELLE – **Je t'aime, t'aime, je t'aime plus que tout**
CHŒURS – **Papapappa**

ELLE – L'amour que nous n'ferons jamais ensem-
Ble est le plus beau, le plus violent
Le plus pur, le plus enivrant
LUI – Exquise esquisse, délicieuse enfant
Ma chair et mon sang
Oh ! mon bébé, mon âme

Chorus

HER - The love we'll never make together
Is the most uncommon, the most troubling
The purest, the rawest[163]
HIM - Exquisite silhouette, luscious child
My flesh and blood
Oh! my baby, my soul

Chorus

HER - The love we'll never make together
Is the most uncommon, the most troubling
The purest, the headiest
HIM - Exquisite silhouette, luscious child
My flesh and blood
Oh! my baby, my soul

HER – Inceste de citron
CHORISTS – Lemon incest
HER – I love you, I love you, love you more than anything
CHORISTS – Papapappa

---

163   A more accurate translation for this verse would be: "the purest, the most moving". However, your translator elected to employ a more compact superlative for the sake of continuity (following the use of "purest").

Refrain

ELLE – L'amour que nous n'ferons jamais ensem-
Ble est le plus rare, le plus troublant
Le plus pur, le plus émouvant
LUI – Exquise esquisse, délicieuse enfant
Ma chair et mon sang
Oh ! mon bébé, mon âme

Refrain

ELLE – L'amour que nous n'ferons jamais ensem-
Ble est le plus rare, le plus troublant
Le plus pur, le plus enivrant
LUI – Exquise esquisse, délicieuse enfant
Ma chair et mon sang
Oh ! mon bébé, mon âme

ELLE – Inceste de citron
CHŒURS – Lemon incest
ELLE – Je t'aime, t'aime, je t'aime plus que tout
CHŒURS – Papapappa

Paroles Serge Gainsbourg
Musique Serge Gainsbourg d'après l'étude Opus 10 n°3 de Chopin
© Melody Nelson Publishing

CHARLOTTE FOR EVER [1986]

Serge directed and wrote the script for the 1986 movie *Charlotte for Ever*[164], in which an alcoholic screenwriter loses his wife and then proceeds to make his daughter the sole object of his affection. The eponymous song is part of the film's soundtrack.

The role of the screenwriter was to be played by Christophe Lambert, but he backed out after initially accepting the part. Serge then decided to step in, with Charlotte still in the daughter's role.* This only served to accentuate the film's incestuous undertones.

The film was evidently very self-reflective and personal for Serge: although not a widower, he was still not over his breakup with Jane. Serge had also been writing scripts from time to time ever since his 1976 film *Je t'aime moi non plus,* a fact that only served to further tie him to the film's main character.

The song's lyrics are set to *Andantino,* a 1926 piece by Soviet-Armenian composer Aram Khachaturian.*

> HIM – Charlotte
> CHORISTS – Charlotte for ever
> HER – My daydreaming daddy
> HIM – Charlotte
> CHORISTS – Charlotte for ever
> HER – Forever in my heart
>
> HIM – Charlotte
> CHORISTS – Charlotte for ever
> HER – Seeking a never
> More… HIM – Is it for ever
> CHORISTS – Charlotte for ever
> HIM – All loves eventually die
>
> **HIM – Without you**
> **I'm no longer me**
> **I drift off to infinity**
> **HER – Feel me**
> **Come closer**[165]
> **Love of my life**
>
> HIM – Charlotte
> CHORISTS – Charlotte for ever
> HER – Outsider love
> HIM – Charlotte
> CHORISTS – Charlotte for ever

---

164 This is how the word "forever" is spelled in the album title, song title, and film title.

165 The original lyrics make clear that "come" is in the imperative form (not tied to the previous verse).

CHARLOTTE FOR EVER

Lui – Charlotte
Chœurs – Charlotte for ever
Elle – Petit papa rêveur
Lui – Charlotte
Chœurs – Charlotte for ever
Elle – À jamais dans mon cœur

Lui – Charlotte
Chœurs – Charlotte for ever
Elle – Recherche d'un never
More... Lui – Est-ce for ever
Chœurs – Charlotte for ever
Lui – Tous les amours se meurent

Lui – Sans toi
Je n'suis plus moi
J'dérive à l'infini
Elle – Sens-moi
Approche-toi
Amour de ma vie

Lui – Charlotte
Chœurs – Charlotte for ever
Elle – Amour outsider
Lui – Charlotte
Chœurs – Charlotte for ever

HIM – No leader, no dealer[166]

HIM – Charlotte
CHORISTS – Charlotte for ever
HER – You authored me
HIM – Charlotte
CHORISTS – Charlotte for ever
HIM – Do you measure up[167]

Chorus

HIM – Charlotte
CHORISTS – Charlotte for ever
HIM – Take pity on me my sweet
Charlotte
CHORISTS – Charlotte for ever
HER – You've won I'm crying

HIM – Charlotte
CHORISTS – Charlotte for ever
HER – Daddy daddy I'm scared
HIM – Charlotte
CHORISTS – Charlotte for ever
HER – To taste your flavor

HIM – Charlotte
CHORISTS – Charlotte for ever
HER – Neither seen nor unseen
HIM – Charlotte
CHORISTS – Charlotte for ever
HER – Corruption of a minor

CHORISTS – Charlotte for ever
Charlotte for ever

---

166   This verse is in English in the original lyrics.

167   Tacitly, this verse seems to read: "Do you measure up to my talent and accomplishments?"
Charlotte would go on to have an extremely successful career in music and acting.

Lui – No leader, no dealer

Lui – Charlotte
Chœurs – Charlotte for ever
Elle – De moi tu es l'auteur
Lui – Charlotte
Chœurs – Charlotte for ever
Lui – Es-tu à la hauteur

Refrain

Lui – Charlotte
Chœurs – Charlotte for ever
Lui – Pitié pour moi mon cœur
Charlotte
Chœurs – Charlotte for ever
Elle – Tu as gagné je pleure

Lui – Charlotte
Chœurs – Charlotte for ever
Elle – Papa papa j'ai peur
Lui – Charlotte
Chœurs – Charlotte for ever
Elle – De goûter ta saveur

Lui – Charlotte
Chœurs – Charlotte for ever
Elle – Vu ni vu, ni couleur
Lui – Charlotte
Chœurs – Charlotte for ever
Lui – Détournement de mineure

Chœurs – Charlotte for ever
Charlotte for ever

Paroles Serge Gainsbourg
Musique Aram Khachaturian
© GPFI / Le Chant du Monde

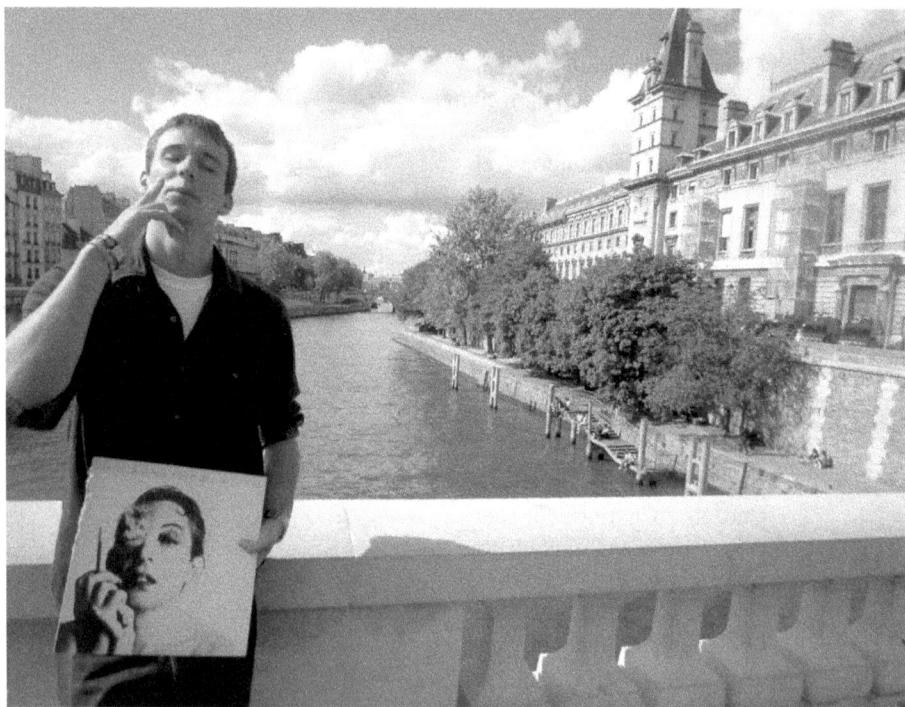

Your translator in 2011 with a copy of Love on the Beat,
on the Pont Saint-Michel in Paris

Photo by Eszter Simor

www.ingramcontent.com/pod-product-compliance
Lightning Source LLC
Chambersburg PA
CBHW070328090426
42733CB00012B/2398